MICHAEL R. CLARKE

EMPLOYMENT STRATEGIES for Today

Idaho State University

Kendall Hunt
publishing company

Kendall Hunt
publishing company

www.kendallhunt.com
Send all inquiries to:
4050 Westmark Drive
Dubuque, IA 52004-1840

ISBN 978-1-4652-6954-6

Printed in the United States of America

Dedication

This book is dedicated to Dr. Frank Clarke, my late father and mentor.

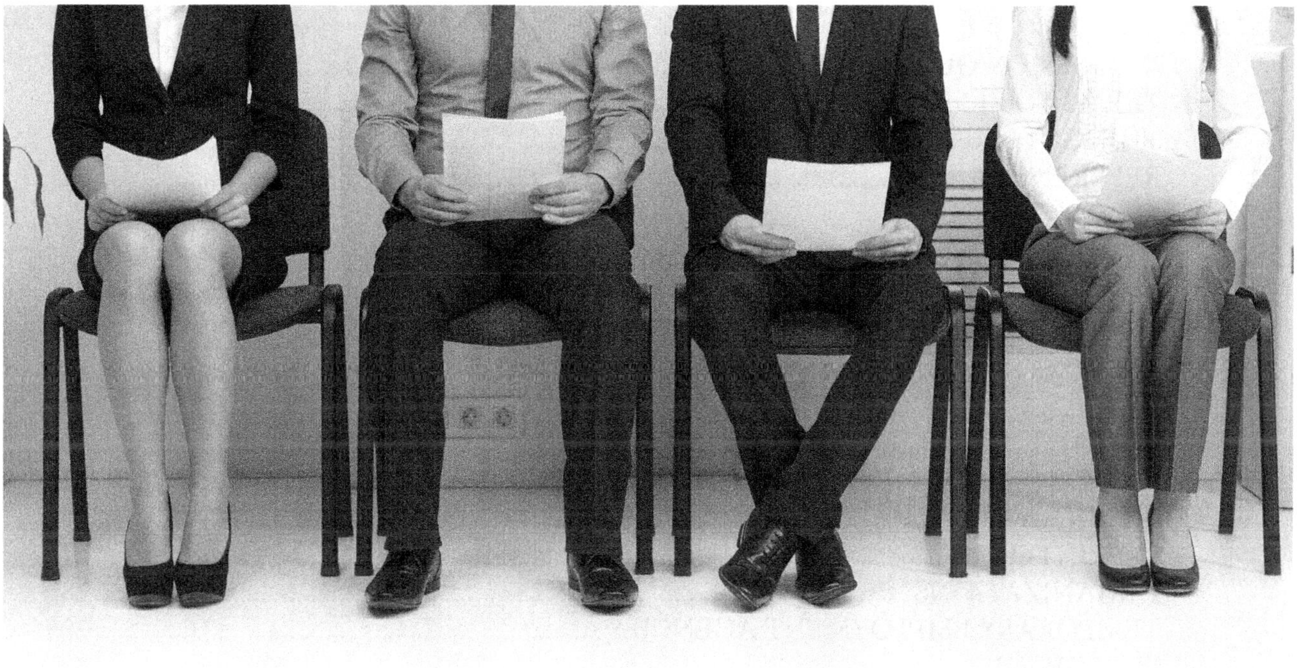

CONTENTS

INTRODUCTION ix

ACKNOWLEDGMENTS xi

ABOUT THE AUTHOR xiii

CHAPTER 1: EASY READING 1

- FUNDAMENTALS 2
- TERMS TO REMEMBER 9
- THINGS TO REMEMBER 9
- REFERENCES 9

CHAPTER 2: THE BASICS 11

- THREE THINGS YOU NEED TO KNOW 12
- WORK, WORK 16
- RESEARCH 20
- AVOID RASH DECISIONS 20

DISCUSSION QUESTIONS 21
TERMS TO REMEMBER 21
THINGS TO REMEMBER 22
REFERENCES 22

CHAPTER 3: NETWORKING: THE WHAT, WHO, WHERE, HOW, AND WHEN 23
WHAT 23
WHO 24
WHERE 24
HOW 25
WHEN 26
VOLUNTEERING 27
ORGANIZATIONS 28
TEMPORARY EMPLOYMENT AGENCIES 29
FOLLOW-UP 30
RESEARCH 30
DISCUSSION QUESTIONS 31
TERMS TO REMEMBER 31
THINGS TO REMEMBER 32
REFERENCES 32

CHAPTER 4: SOCIAL MEDIA AND YOUR JOB CAMPAIGN 33
SOCIAL MEDIA IN SCHOOLS 34
TERMS YOU NEED TO KNOW 36
HOW TO USE SOCIAL MEDIA 37
HOW EMPLOYERS USE SOCIAL MEDIA 37
LINKEDIN 38
DISCUSSION QUESTIONS 41
TERMS TO REMEMBER 42
THINGS TO REMEMBER 42
REFERENCES 42

CHAPTER 5: RESUMES 43
MAKE OR BREAK 43
KINDS OF RESUMES 44
CHRONOLOGICAL RESUME 47
FUNCTIONAL RESUMES 49
DISCUSSION QUESTIONS 52
TERMS TO REMEMBER 52
THINGS TO REMEMBER 52

CHAPTER 6: COVER LETTERS AND REFERENCES 53
COVER LETTERS 53
WHAT GOES WHERE 59
SAMPLE COVER LETTERS 60
REFERENCES 60
DISCUSSION QUESTIONS 63
TERMS TO REMEMBER 63
THINGS TO REMEMBER 63
REFERENCES 63

CHAPTER 7: STANDARD INTERVIEW 65
HOW IT WORKS 65
EARLY BIRDS 68
BOTTOM LINE 69
THE END 72
DISCUSSION QUESTIONS 73
TERMS TO REMEMBER 74
THINGS TO REMEMBER 74

CHAPTER 8: BEHAVIORAL INTERVIEW 75
SOFT SKILLS 76
THE REAL YOU 76
MY INFORMAL POLL 78
PHONE INTERVIEWS 81
PITFALLS 83
CODE OF CONDUCT 83
DISCUSSION QUESTIONS 84
TERMS TO REMEMBER 85
THINGS TO REMEMBER 85

CHAPTER 9: HOW TO KEEP THE JOB 87
CUSTOMER SERVICE 87
MOTIVATION 88
GROUPS 89
TEAM BUILDING 89
GROUP ROLES 92
MEETINGS 92
DISCUSSION QUESTION 94
TERMS TO REMEMBER 94

THINGS TO REMEMBER 94
REFERENCES 94

CHAPTER 10: DIVERSITY, ETHICS, AND LEADERSHIP 95

DIVERSITY AND MULTICULTURALISM 95
A FEW RULES 95
AREAS OF CONFLICT 96
NONVERBAL COMMUNICATION 97
ETHICS 99
LEADERSHIP 101
DISCUSSION QUESTIONS 103
TERMS TO REMEMBER 103
THINGS TO REMEMBER 103
REFERENCES 103

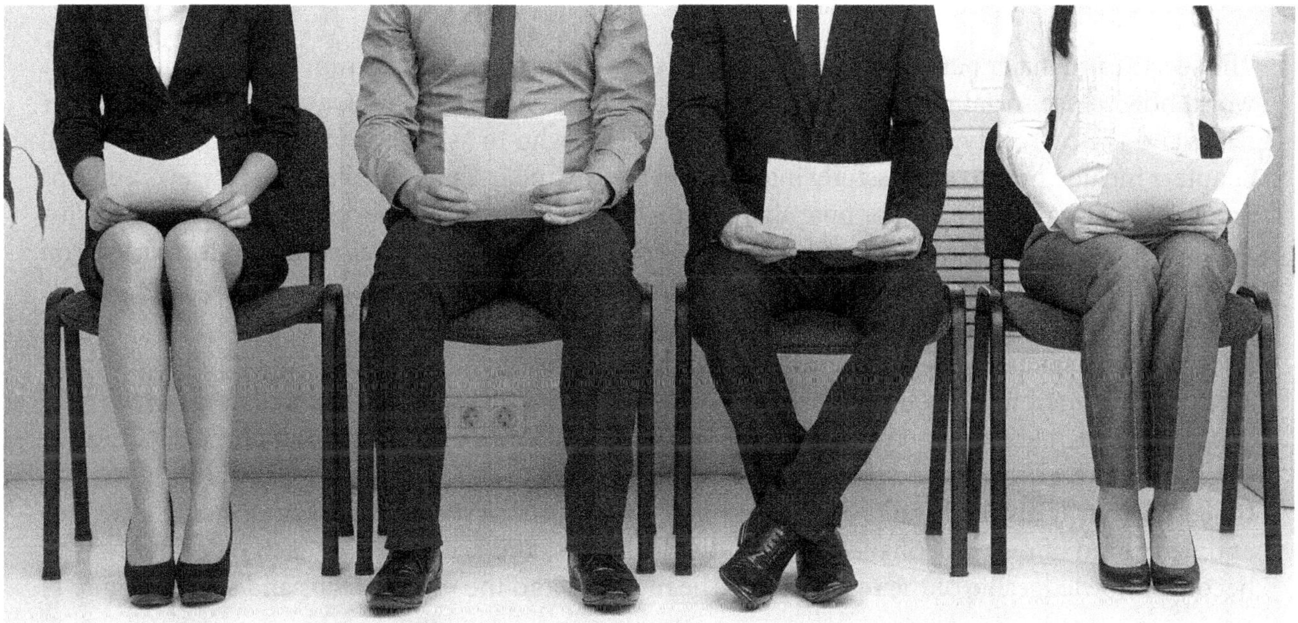

INTRODUCTION

In some ways this book is about only you, and you getting the job you want and need. It's about exploring more of you, and you making the decisions and answering questions that only you can answer. The unique you.

I wrote this book because there are no books that address the questions and answers my students needed to learn, to make the basic decisions of their own individual needs and then how to apply that knowledge in getting a job. My teaching career spans 16 years in the high school, junior college, and (now) university levels. During this time, I've learned that, individually, we all need to answer the questions of how to balance our human needs with the steps of getting a job, and keeping it.

I wrote this book to answer your basic questions about employment strategies. This more comprehensive book is needed to encourage you, the student, to examine more closely what you want and then to teach the basics of how to get a job and keep it in today's job market, which is most definitely not your parents' workplace.

A basic text on getting a job must address two major issues. The first must include your individual needs, your resources, your realities, and answering basic questions like where you want to live and the kind of people you want to work with—that is, the realities of your human needs.

The second and major part involves the essentials of getting a job. This section discusses how to network, how to use social media networking and recognize its pitfalls. A chapter on writing a cover letter and the correct type of resume is here, as well as who to ask for a reference. Two additional chapters include how to successfully interview in both standard and behavioral interviews and tips on what and what not to do. The final chapters include keeping a job by exploring cultural diversity, team inclusion, leadership roles, and customer service. Each chapter gives you the information you will need to secure and retain your job choice for your successful chosen career.

Each chapter stands alone. If you need a cover letter or a resume, this book provides the essential areas of information. Do you need help to review what job you want or where you want to live? Do you need help in learning networking skills that do not alienate or irritate other people? This book covers basics and essentials needed for today's job market, such as how to make career decisions based on your individual wants and needs; how to discover new and easy ways to write a resume and what kind of resume enhances your individual skills, and the pitfalls of each type; and how to become knowledgeable of the resources on the internet, and the inserted tabs and supplements.

Welcome. I invite you to discover the basics of getting the job you want and need, for right now, for the unique you.

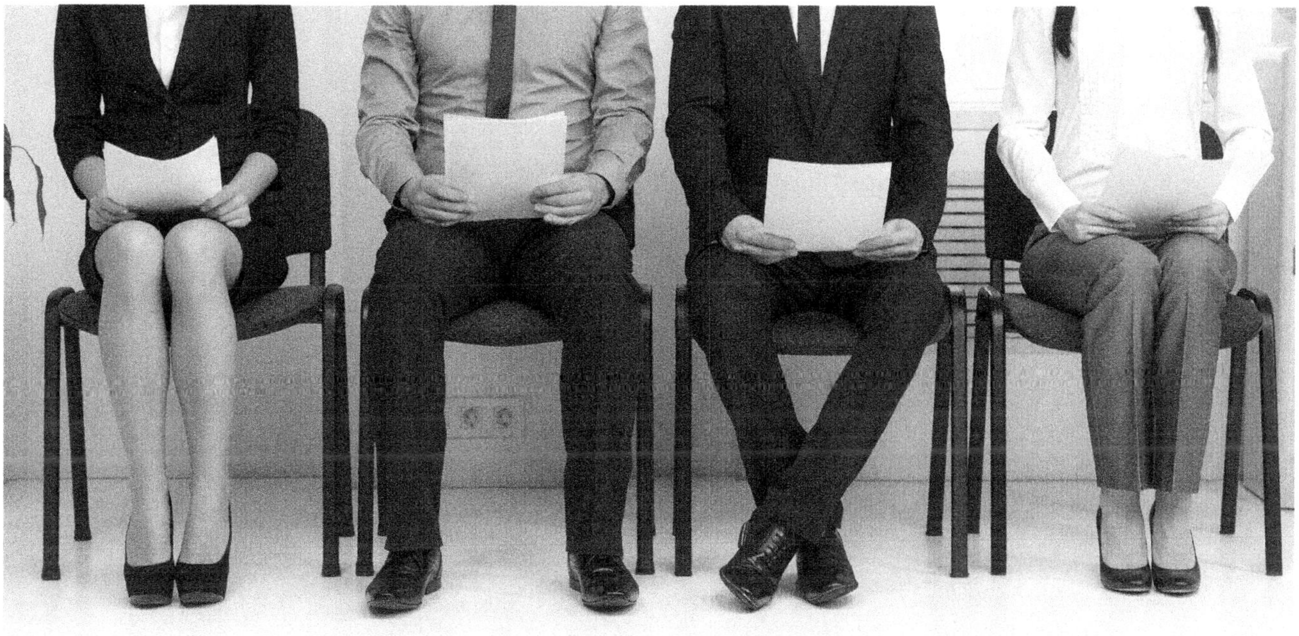

ACKNOWLEDGMENTS

I would like to thank my friends and colleagues for their advice and stories. I would like to thank Idaho State University's College of Technology for allowing me the opportunity to teach here and for the rich and supportive work environment, especially Dean Scott Rasmussen, my Department Chair Teena Rhoads, and my coordinator Clayn Lambert. I would also like to thank my family—special thanks to Pearl Clarke for being my sounding board and keeping me halfway sane. For all those I have not mentioned, thank you. On this journey, I have learned a little from all of you.

Michael Clarke
clarmic8@isu.edu

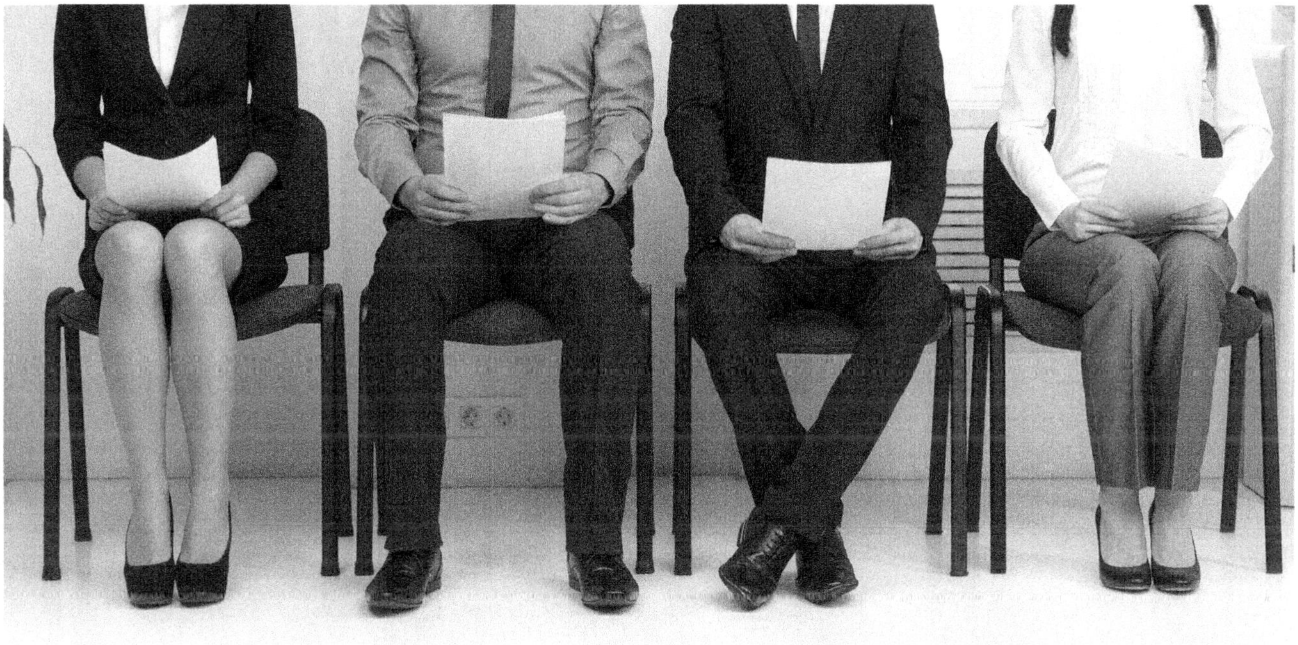

ABOUT THE AUTHOR

Michael attended Idaho State University from 1982 to 1984. He received his B.S. in Business with a Finance concentration from California Polytechnic State University in San Luis Obispo in 1992. Before and after graduating college, he worked in and on various disciplines including Real Estate Finance, Network Administration, and consulting in the Retail, Medical, and Computer sectors.

In 2001, he received his Single Subject Teaching Credential at Fresno Pacific University. He also worked as an adjunct instructor in the Business Division for 10 years at College of the Sequoias in Visalia, California, teaching Marketing, Microsoft Office, Web Design, Sales, Business English as well as serving as Director of the Entrepreneurship Program.

In 2008 he received his Masters of Business Administration. He worked at the College of the Sequoias and Willow International College in Clovis, California, before coming to work at Idaho State University College of Technology for the 2012-2013 school year. He teaches Workplace Relations, Employment Strategies, and Learning Strategies. He also sits on the Parking Board, the College of Technology Social Committee, and has worked with the "I love ISU" campaign.

He enjoys reading and hiking as well as bicycling in his spare time.

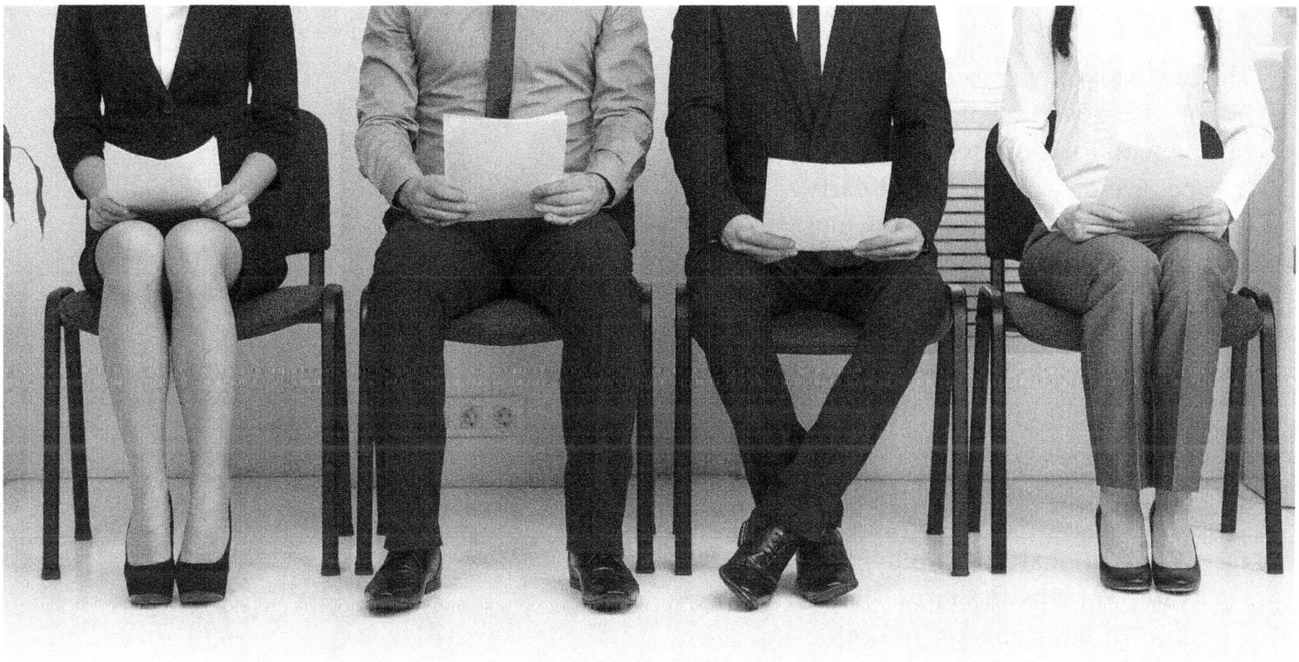

CHAPTER 1

EASY READING

So you're either looking for a job or you're graduating. This book is written so that anyone who needs help with employment strategies can use it. Its basic purpose is to help people from students to professionals in obtaining and keeping employment. Each chapter stands alone; that is, if you only need the resume section, it is contained in the chapter.

While you are reading this book, I will try to give examples and charts including some videos to help with the process. Sometimes I will even tell jokes. Remember to laugh when your instructor tells a joke as your grade may depend on it. Just kidding.

Looking for a job can be stressful and hard. In today's economy, the job search is even harder. Many people are out of work or working in jobs that are below their skills level. This creates tension and stress for many people. The aim of this book is to help you in finding not only a job, but the right job for you. I myself have been through many different jobs and many different occupations, which gives me a unique insight on the stresses and ins and outs of the job search. We will explore the different aspects of the job search, and give you helpful hints and tricks on how to get the job you want. (Note: this will not always be the job you think you deserve.)

The unemployment rate is computed by the U.S. government. It gives the rate of people making jobless claims, irrespective of which political party is in office. It includes the following:

Rawpixel/Shutterstock, Inc.

- The number of people in the **labor force**. This measure is the sum of the employed and the unemployed. In other words, the labor force level is the number of people who are either working or actively seeking work.
- The national **unemployment rate**. Perhaps the most widely known labor market indicator, this statistic reflects the number of unemployed people as a percentage of the labor force.
- The **labor force participation rate**. This measure is the number of people in the labor force as a percentage of the civilian noninstitutional population 16 years old and over. In other words, it is the percentage of the population that is either working or actively seeking work.
- The **employment-population ratio**. This measure is the number of employed as a percentage of the civilian noninstitutionalized population 16 years old and over. In other words, it is the percentage of the population that is currently working.

FUNDAMENTALS

NOW TO GET A JOB

Now you need to develop a strategy to become one of those people who are employed, not an easy achievement in today's job market. There are things to help you accomplish getting that job you want. There are a few fundamentals to remember.

ATTITUDE

Your attitude will make or break you when you are searching for a job. A defeatist attitude will be self-actualizing. If you think you can't, you're right, you probably can't. A half-hearted approach to job searching won't cut it in this economy either, any more than a half-hearted approach to school will get you that A. Employers immediately pick up on attitude, either negative or positive; they're smart and trained to weed out, or in, potential employees.

No matter how you feel on any day, when you meet people, whether you think they can help you find employment or not, having a confident and positive attitude is essential. And *everyone* has the potential to help you. The little old lady down the street who you say "good morning" to has the possibility to mention "that nice young person down the street who would be a great employee for you" to someone else who has an impending job opening. Get your qualifications and job skills out there. Stop for a moment and do your "elevator pitch" (explained later), and she will not only remember your niceness, but also mention you in her large social system that is not within your sphere to access. Also remember to give credit where credit is due for your past accomplishments. You didn't get educated, have skills, or develop as a person without help from many sources. Mention those people when chatting with others. Not only is it thoughtful but it is also a good business practice. All people want to be recognized and valued; this win-win costs very little.

Ollyy/Shutterstock, Inc.

Successful people have a sense of self-worth. I said self-worth, not self-importance. Many people, especially those who have done really well in academics, have a feeling of entitlement. A "oh, I know all there is to know about that subject" attitude. There is a not so fine line between confidence and arrogance. Confidence is a belief in one's own abilities while arrogance is one of conceit. There is nothing that turns off a prospective employer faster than a show of arrogance because those people are difficult to lead even when their skills set would be of value to the company. As one of my old bosses used to say, "My company. My rules. You do it my way. Period." Employers don't have time, energy, or inclination to put up with crap and they don't have to; there are plenty of other people to choose from.

What you really want employers to know is that you are a thoughtful team player, willing and capable of working with a variety of other personalities. You want them to know that you are a self-starter and will work hard to make their company/organization better. You must articulate the fact that you are willing to do whatever they need you to do and that you expect to work your way up in the company. They want to know if you're being honest with them on your resume, interview, and chatting; many a career has been destroyed by exaggeration. For example, let's say you exaggerate your past jobs or say, "I am a veteran" when you're not. This may get you an interview and a firing when the truth comes out. Which it will, eventually.

This is also the time to be honest with yourself by way of a self-analysis. Ask yourself: Why would someone want to hire me? What do I do especially well? For many, it's that they have the personality to get along with anyone; they are color-blind, gender-blind, ethnicity-blind. For others it may be that activities in their personal life can co-mingle with job requirements for a good employment fit. A list of questions to help with this is at the end of the chapter. Remember, you are responsible for yourself. You need to become your own advocate; this mean you do not depend on your parents, friends, or teachers. The job will be yours so the job hunting is also yours. No one knows you better than you.

Doing a job that gives you satisfaction makes you better at the job and is crucial to being a good employee. This self-reflection can be painful especially if someone important in your life has chosen a different career path for you. If your father is an accountant and you are drawn to a career in music, it may be difficult to choose your heart's calling. This may take you to look at your own wants, a step that is often necessary for self-motivation. If you hate your job, or are at least lukewarm toward it, in time you become a rotten employee.

Employers don't care about your life story.

Comodo777/Shutterstock, Inc.

This will come as a shock to many job seekers but employers do not care if your life story thus far is miserable. *What they do care about is how you handle adversity and if you can help the company make more profits.* When a crisis comes, and it always does, your behavior at that moment deeply affects the company. An employer will ponder: "Would this person fall apart or could he lead toward a new solution? Does she think creatively? What is his work ethic? Will we be able to work together constructively? Will she fit into the team and be an asset? Will his skills enhance those of the people already here?"

The only other reason an employer would be interested in your distressing life story is in turning you down because you have too many stressors in your life. There are other people who have the same skills you have and can devote more of their energies toward the boss's business. Sounds cold and unfeeling? The job of a hiring committee is to sign the employee who has the most skills and/or potential for the company. Period. Employers want to know how you can help them increase or maintain their bottom line. It is sad that you got laid off and that your twin sisters are ill, but employers want you to leave all the baggage at home and concentrate on what you can do for them. Oh, and they want you to be enthusiastic while you're doing it. And "I really need a job" doesn't cut it either.

Putting in the time

Treat looking for a job as a job—a real job. This is not a vacation. Get up and get dressed at a time that you would normally go to work, say 8 a.m. Plan out your day and actively seek employment until 5 p.m. Check out different online sources that may have changed since the last time you looked. Call those old friends and talk with them about how they got their job. (See how to network the right way in Chapter 3 of this book.)

The more time you put into looking for employment the better chance you have of finding it. This is the time in your life when you need to step up to the plate and become self-directed, which is a hard lesson to learn. There are people and companies looking for motivated employees but they don't come knocking on doors nor do a lot of them advertise (they don't have to; they receive referrals from their employees and interesting resumes). According to a recent article in the *Wall Street Journal*, only 20% of jobs are advertised. This will depend on your field of course, but consider this: "While the Internet has made it easy to apply for work, career experts say that offline networking efforts to meet people and get introductions are a far more effective way to land jobs—especially since 80% of jobs aren't publicly advertised, says Steven Rothberg, founder of job-search website CollegeRecruiter.com in Minneapolis" (Nishi, 2013). What you need to be is one of those referrals—someone who knows your abilities and is willing to recommend you to their boss. Again, this means calling everyone from your Great-Aunt Susie to your old boss. Be sure to use the elevator pitch rather than a direct confrontational style. The elevator pitch will be explained in detail in the Interviewing chapters.

BPTU/Shutterstock, Inc.

What else you'll need

Some other things you'll need as you begin your job search are:

1. Research. You will need to do research on the specific job you're applying for. Gone are the days when you created one resume and cover letter and made 50 copies of it on resume paper. This goes back to the days of typewriters. Now with computers and word processing programs, you need to target each and every job and do the research. This means, as we'll talk more about in the cover letter and resume chapters, you tailor each resume and cover letter for the specific job you're applying for. You will also be doing research on the company you're applying for so you can talk intelligently about its successes.
2. Cover letter and references. Although some companies no longer require a cover letter, most companies ask for them. A well-written letter is your key to the front door of a company and one of the keys to getting an interview. As with everything else related to getting a job, it needs to be polished and perfect (more to come in the cover letter chapter). Also, start thinking about who you might want to use as professional references. No family members, no friends, no classmates, and no roommates are to be used. Your references should be people who can speak of your professionalism. A former boss (if you know he or she will say good things about you) is okay, as is a former teacher or professor. Avoid using your church leaders, as that gets into the aspects of religion, which is a federally protected right to privacy. Last but not

Login/Shutterstock, Inc.

least, make sure you contact your references and let them know you are using them! I just love getting a call out of the blue about a former student (yes, that's sarcasm)! But, if they send me an email or give me a call and ask politely if they can use me as a reference, I usually don't mind. When I'm hiring someone, I want the references to tell me something timely and appropriate about the applicant, so choose wisely.

3. Resume. This is a document that represents you. Let me say that again: this document represents you. It has to be perfect! Skills need to be updated, education section clear, former jobs listed concisely.

   Remember, most of the time, potential hirers have not met you nor do they know how wonderful you are. The resume represents you and gets you the interview! Just as most of your future employers don't want you making mistakes, they don't want someone with an "I don't give a ______!" attitude about their resume. Mistakes are mistakes. Much more in the resume chapter!
4. Social media and career networking. We will talk about all this in the proper chapters.
5. Interviews and their types. There are two types of interviews, standard and behavioral. We'll talk about them and how to answer the questions in those chapters.
6. Self-confidence. I'M AWESOME! Well, of course you are! Now you just have to prove it! What I want you to do is create a folder on your computer. Name it, "I'm Awesome." Or get a manila folder and write "I'm Awesome" on it. Go ahead, I'll wait.

Login/Shutterstock, Inc.

Okay, got it? Now I want you to think about your previous resumes (if you had one), cover letters, and references. All of them go into the folder. Think about that paper you got an A on, that lab project you enjoyed, that competition you entered and placed in, that dean's list you made, or whatever else you're proud of and put it in there. Now, when you are ready to start writing, you also have all the information you will need at your fingertips. While you're at it, go to your course catalog or transcript, and print or copy that in there, too. You'll probably need that along the way! The next section provides some questions you can ask yourself while getting your "I'm Awesome" file ready. I strongly recommend you start writing the answers to these questions down so they are in your folder when you need them. Want to just answer them in your head? Don't! You never know when in the middle of an interview your mind will go blank and you'll need to have it written down.

PathDoc/Shutterstock, Inc.

List of "the basics" or what you need to ask yourself before you take a job leading to a career

What are your goals? Long-term job outlook? Short-term job outlook? Stepping stones? What kind of job are you looking for?
Answers to these questions will make a tremendous difference in your search. Being on the lookout for a job that is part time is a small thing compared to that career job you are looking for when you graduate.

Spare time? Hobbies?
What do you like to do in your spare time? Nobody can work 24/7, so you need to think about what recreation is available in the area where you are job searching. If you like to hunt and fish, a job in New York City is probably not going to fit those needs.

Setting? Do you want to work in an office or work outside?
This is not a random question that you can say, "Oh, anything is fine." You will be working at this place all day or night. If you enjoy working outside, make sure that is what you do.

What kind of people do you want to work with?
You need to make sure you get along with the people you work with. When you are interviewing, make sure they are a right fit for you also. If you are a fairly serious type, and they play a lot of practical jokes, that is probably not the right firm for you, and vice versa.

Cost management minus pay—can I afford the place?
Does the job pay well for the area where you will be living (a teacher in a large city in California versus a small Iowa town)? If you want to be a teacher and work in a large city, you might find the costs of living to be high; however, if the idea of working in a small town appeals to you, the salary versus cost of living might be more in your favor.

What other impacts should you consider?
Where you work is going to affect the rest of your life, from social life to clothes. Does the area have enough social things for you to do? If it is a small town and you like to go out at night, then social options could be limited. Do you like to dress sharp? Does your job require you to work in overalls? That will not work. Again, make sure they match, for you and them.

List of abilities and skills

Mmaxer/Shutterstock, Inc.

This is NOT the time to be modest, yet be honest. Start now creating a list of your best abilities and skills. Ask yourself:

What accomplishment am I the most proud of? What was that skill?

What skills have I learned in my classes I've taken (these will probably be the most important)? What computer skills do I have? What software programs am I competent in?

Do I have the ability to communicate in writing?

Do I have volunteer work that transfers to this job?

Have I given presentations to large groups of people?

What was my best skill in my most recent job? In my personal life?

Do I work well within a team or do I prefer to be the Lone Ranger without Tonto?

What business/place would be a good fit for me? Big or small?

What was my most creative job? Or unusual skill?

Have I ever mentored or trained someone?

Do I have good customer service skills? Phone answering?

List of commendations and awards

These listings will all be personal, but don't forget things like:

High school awards
Scouting awards
Athletic scholarships
Club awards

You get the idea, anything and everything you think might help and can be put into your I'M AWESOME folder belongs there.

TERMS TO REMEMBER

Handicaps	Paycheck	Life work
Spare time	Communalities	Risks

THINGS TO REMEMBER

- There are no right or wrong answers to what I want.
- If it's to be it's up to me.
- Work aspects are not carved in stone; you will change and grow.
- Finding where you fit is a goal.

REFERENCE

Nishi, D. (2013, May 28). Soft skills can help you get ahead. Retrieved November 17, 2014, from http://www.wsj.com/articles/SB10001424127887324715704578481290888822474w.wsj.com/news/articles/SB10001424127887323869604578368733437346820?-mod=e2fb&mg=reno64-wsj&url=http%3A%2F%2Fonline.wsj.com%2Farticle%2FSB10001424127887323869604578368733437346820.html%3Fmod%3De2fb

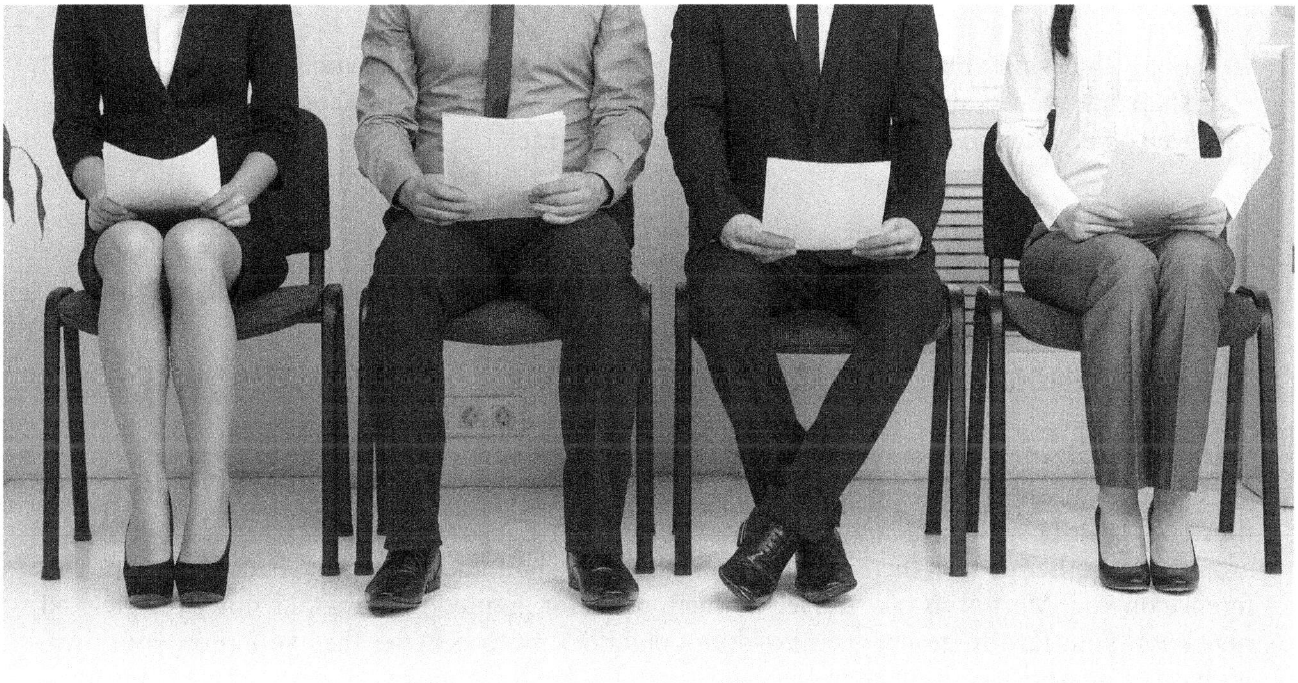

CHAPTER 2

THE BASICS

First, and most important for this chapter, is that there are no "right" answers. It's more of a question of, "What do you want?" Nobody is you but you and only you can make the *want* decisions. (Notice it does not say the "right" decision.) Your mom or girlfriend or significant other or the next-door neighbor can tell you what to do but only you can tell what you ***want and need for your happiness.*** Whether you are 18 or 48 if you are reading this book, you are looking for change. I can hear many of you say, "but, but, but …" There are a lot of buts out there. Now you're probably thinking; but if I do this, so and so will think I'm crazy. Or worse yet, not like me. Get over it, Bud. This is not high school or third grade anymore. Why the heck do you care about what others think? You are a grown-up or at least almost so. What you do is up to you. I thought I would leave this area with a top-five list.

1. It isn't fair, oh well; suck it up and keep going.
2. Laundry always builds up. It doesn't magically disappear.
3. Your problems don't matter to me. While I can empathize, I really have problems of my own.
4. Your excuses don't matter. I used the same ones when I was your age, and they didn't work then either.
5. One day you will have the same problems your parents have. It is a fact of life that we get more responsibilities as we get older. If you think you are crushed by life now, wait. It gets worse.

5a. Enjoy this while you can. Sure parents are a pain, school's a bother, and life is depressing. But someday you'll realize how wonderful it was to be a kid. Maybe you should start now. You're welcome. **Okay so there were five and a half, sue me.**

THREE THINGS YOU NEED TO KNOW

1. Know You for Now

One of the basics you must remember is that who you were yesterday is not the same person as you are today. I know it sounds trite but it's true. If you've been alone for the last 24 hours then your mind has been busy with thoughts—analyzing, discarding, and accepting. If you've been hanging around with other people, their behavior, conversations, and interactions have made a subtle difference on you. Most of us take ourselves much more for granted than we take other people. You may know your favorite teacher or next-door neighbor's motives better than you know your own. It's hard to question yourself; and it's oh so easy to lie. We lie to ourselves all the time: "This piece of pie doesn't really have 400 gazillion calories in it." or "This house won't really cost me 70% of my income." Worse yet, "My talents are so outstanding that someone wonderful out there in the world will recognize them." NOT, NOPE, WHAT ARE YOU THINKING? The people who do make it (read get what they want) work toward that goal; be it a musician or a certified nursing assistant. They get training, take tests, and generally practice their skills until their dream is everyday life. Whether that dream becomes a reality or not is up to each of us.

A short story:
Our family has the good fortune to acquire good educations mainly because our father felt that education was the way UP. We have had to work our butts off to get where we are. None of us has been able to say, "It's not fair, so and so has it so much easier!" The one reason we cannot do that is our role model, our father.

So, the story starts with a young Hualapai Indian boy sent to Sherman Institute, a Native American boarding school. There he learns basic skills like carpentry and auto mechanics. You know, skills for someone like him to aspire to, after all, not much is expected of him. He knows there is nothing wrong with these skills; he just wants to do something different. So, after graduating, he moves to Los Angeles and works as a janitor at night and goes to Los Angeles City College by day; he has no financial help at all. When he is 20 years old Pearl Harbor was bombed, and he immediately left school to join the Navy. He spent over two years on a troop transport ship in the Pacific Ocean, taking wounded Marines off the Solomon, including Guadalcanal. As a medical corpsman, he developed a living blood bank for his ship, and the Navy sent him back to college at UCLA to pursue pre-med studies in the V-12 program. While at UCLA he played football for the first time in him life because making the team meant tutors and steak dinners. He attended medical school working nights as an extern while going to school during the day, and then re-joined the Navy in time for the Korean Conflict and for several years after as a Navy doc.

He then practiced medicine in the small town of Woodlake in the central valley of California for many years delivering medical care, delivering babies and working as a team physician. In later years he was recruited by the Public Health Service, Indian Health Service where he served for eleven years as a hospital medical director. He returned to Woodlake to private practice again and eventually retired. He returned to the practice of medicine in his eighties to donate one day a week to a free clinic until he was 91 years old.

None of us six kids will ever top that.

sergey causelove/Shutterstock, Inc.

2. You Will Grow and Change

The second thing you need to know is that you will grow and change. It's not unusual for a college freshman to change his or her major three or more times. I started in psychology and ended up graduating in finance. Some of the subjects are totally new, others offer a new slant. It's not only okay but I urge you to experiment. Take a class in something that interests you, something you would never think of—now is the time to explore. Even after you get a job in your career path you may want to change directions. My father told me that in a new job:

> The first year you learn about the expectations.
> The second year you start implementing your ideas.
> The third year you finish executing changes.
> The fourth year you finish putting your ideas into operations.

And from then on you coast.

Some very smart people go back to school every four years or broaden their goals or move up the ladder or do a 180 into something entirely new.

3. Love Your Lifetime Work

The third thing you need to know is that you must love your lifetime work. We all take jobs that we have to take because we need to eat and pay rent. Sometimes these jobs are temporary and sometimes they lead to something more permanent. Joe took a short-term job in a pizza shop and found he loved the interaction with different kinds of people. He went back to junior college at night hoping for a manager's job. Long story short, he now owns four pizza shops in little towns around the area. And he thought his dream job would be to work with computers. Go figure. What he hadn't taken into consideration was that he was a people-person. Sitting in a cubicle staring at a screen all day would have eventually bored him to tears.

Which are you? Do you want to work directly with people, only peripherally, or not at all? Patsy works from home imputing data for a medical billing service. She sees few people with her work but has an active community life. Compromise.

AND YOU?

Now the biggie: What do you want? What is practical and what is the dream for now? Next month it might change but for now, What is your dream? When you were very young someone was always asking you what you wanted to be when you grew up. I went through the fireman–policeman–professional athlete stage. Then life happened. Some things were out of reach (I loved baseball but my desire was not adequate for a professional player). Now, the real world has demands that need to be met.

Sunny studio/Shutterstock, Inc.

Abraham Maslow's hierarchy of needs comes into play here. Maslow was a psychologist who in 1943 developed a pyramid-shaped model to explain the human psyche. He created a five-step pyramid (see below). Maslow stated that first we must take care of certain needs before the other needs can be met. First, we must take care of the bottom rung before you can climb up the ladder. The bottom rung consists of the basic needs such as food and shelter, breathing, and safety. Without these needs, we cannot try for anything else. Think about it, if you do not have air to breathe, water to drink, clothing, and a safe place to eat, how can you think of anything else? These basic needs must be met before anything else. Sometimes we take jobs to sustain ourselves and our loved ones. No matter what the job is, we have to bite the bullet and do it until we can reach for that next step—the security step. Once we have the basics, we then move on to the next step, safety and security.

In this second stage, we look for something to guide us. For many people, this is family, health, and employment. These things guide us and fulfill psychological needs in us. Humans are basically social animals, and as such, we need to be around people who are similar to us. We achieve these with our personal property, our jobs, and by hanging out with people who are similar to us.

The third stage is where we seek love and belonging. We are not talking about your true love here. We are more talking about our need to be loved. This comes from our families, our friends, and our connections to fellow human beings. Unless you are a hermit, you are around other people—some you love, some you tolerate, others you may genuinely dislike. It does not matter for our purposes. Think of when you were a child and made friends. It did not matter who they were, we didn't think of what color, social status, or whatever made them different from us. In many ways, children lead us in this category. All they want is our love and praise, not our differences. In our complicated world today, it would be nice if we could return to these values, wouldn't it? Instead, adult life is complicated but we still need that sense of belonging. This is why clubs such as Rotary, Lions, Elks, etc., are so popular—they touch that sense of belonging we need.

The fourth stage is where most people end up. This is the self-esteem stage. Again, humans need to fulfill all of the lower stages to get to this stage, which is where we start to be recognized for our achievements. Think about those little certificates you received for something you did, or those trophies from scouting. Admit it, you probably still have those somewhere, don't you? We all like those little things. We like those little pats on the back, when your boss or teacher tells you, "Good job!" It's a small thing, but it feels good. Within this stage rests our confidence, achievements, our need to be recognized. This is one of the reasons we climb that metaphorical ladder to success—sure, more money doesn't hurt, but being someone who sets a goal and achieves it feels good.

Unfortunately, most of us will never reach the fifth step, self-actualization. Self-actualization is as hard to explain as it is to achieve, so I will let Maslow (1962) explain it: "The growth of self-actualization refers to the need for personal growth and discovery that is present throughout a person's life." For Maslow, a person is always "becoming" and never remains static in these terms. In self-actualization we come to find a meaning to life that is important to us.

As each person is unique the motivation for self-actualization leads people in different directions (Kenrick et al., 2010). For some people self-actualization can be achieved through creating works of art or literature, for others through sport, in the classroom, or within a corporate setting.

Maslow (1962) believed self-actualization could be measured through the concept of peak experiences. This occurs when a person experiences the world totally for what it is, and there are feelings of euphoria, joy, and wonder.

It is important to note that self-actualization is a continual process of becoming rather than a perfect state one reaches of a "happy ever after" (Hoffman, 1988).

Maslow offers the following description of self-actualization:

> It refers to the person's desire for self-fulfillment, namely, to the tendency for him to become actualized in what he is potentially.
>
> The specific form that these needs will take will of course vary greatly from person to person. In one individual it may take the form of the desire to be an ideal mother, in another it may be expressed athletically, and in still another it may be expressed in painting pictures or in inventions (Maslow, 1943, pp. 382–383).

So, where are you in this pyramid? It is hard to explain, isn't it? What step are you on? Where have you been in the past? All of these are worthy questions to ask yourself. A little growth won't hurt you, I swear it won't.

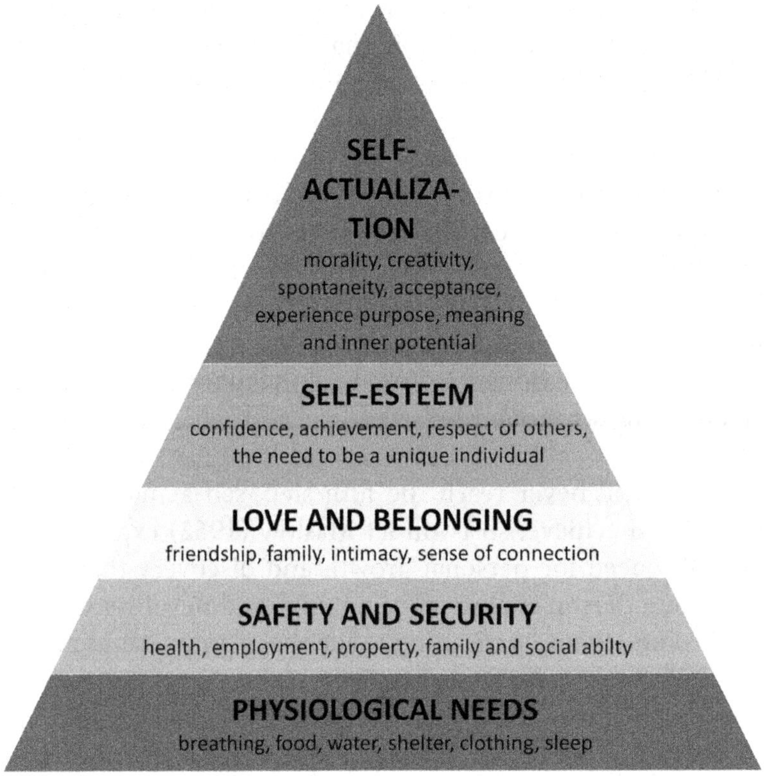

Elenarts/Shutterstock, Inc.

This means that all of us are growing and changing...

WORK, WORK

JOB OR CAREER?

Now, about that job, is it for a temporary measure or as a long-term, possibly upper mobile career movement, or something in between? Do you have a choice or are finances so tight that any job has to be taken to pay the rent? How serious it is depends on how much responsibility you have in your life. Supporting someone else limits some options for employment but also gives many people stability and a support system that they need during a stressful time.

rungrote/Shuttestock, Inc.

Whether it's temporary or semi-permanent may also include your age and the risks you are willing to take. Are you willing to move to Seattle and sleep on your friend's couch? Take a creative job and work all the hours needed for success in an innovative workplace? An acquaintance does diesel computerized mechanics and travels throughout the Southwest. A good friend is a makeup artist for Hollywood movies and is gone on locations for weeks, or months, at a time. There's a boatload of problems when travel is a job requirement; missing lots of family and community activities just touches on the difficulties. Could you do that? Some mid-management positions require their employees to move as they progress upward on the corporate ladder. Is that for you?

Family

Monkey Business Images/Shutterstock, Inc.

Do you need family nearby? Note I said need, not want; these are two very different things. Want is to desire, while need is a necessity. If your idea of a perfect Sunday is dinner at Mom's with lots of family and friends, then moving may not work for you. If, however, you are an independent soul whose belief is that seeing family at Christmas is great, moving might be more acceptable. Some families are so enmeshed in their adult children's lives that it impedes personal and career growth. Others are more like associates; they do their own thing until they are needed—like a consultant. You have to find a job and happiness without depending on other people. (One good thing is if a move doesn't work, the road goes both ways, you can always move back.)

Significant other

Another priority that may have to be considered is your significant other, whoever that is. A young physician, Joseph G. chose to work at a hospital in Gallup, New Mexico, where his cardiology talents were badly needed. His fiancé was less enthusiastic about the move, as her master's degree was in Chinese literature. Their tenure did not last long because her work requirements could not be met. He had to move to a location that would also meet some of her needs or part ways. He chose to move to a large eastern city. Another friend, Tony C., moved back to the small town where he grew up taking over a small family farm. His city-bred wife, Ann, was at a loss dealing with the nuances of small-town living and ultimately hated it. She left, he stayed. Their wants and needs were too broad to bridge. Talk before making decisions, not after. It has to work for both people.

Where do I want to live?

Before you can make up your mind as to what size city you want to live in, you have to answer the question, "Do I want to work outside or inside?" If you have your heart set on being a farmer, dairyman, pest control operator, or anything that requires a lot of time spent outdoors, you have to take into consideration what the daily job is like. A friend, Don, owns a small window washing service in a large city; he says he compromised with the need to work outside and the want to own a business. Compromise is not really a four-letter work; sometimes it gives everyone a chance to be who they are.

There's also the factor of the kind of people you want to work with. You are going to spend most of your waking hours with colleagues; liking them could make it more pleasant. If you have nothing in common, this will become problematic, as you will have to spend several hours a day together. This could compromise your work ethics, morality, or integrity; this could cause your job satisfaction to be questionable and your ultimate principles may be on the line. For example, taking small items home might not affect your co-workers' idea of honesty but it might put you in a moral dilemma to report them or not. Choose to work with people who have the basic values you do. Not people particular of your skin color, or background but whose ideas do not conflict with yours. Most people's social life revolves around their co-workers. It makes good sense as these are the people you see every day and know best. These are the people who impact everything from what clothes you wear to some of your knowledge of the world around you (or lack thereof).

Some jobs can best be done in a large city, for example, computerized drafting and advertising. Most computer companies are located in large cities where they have a plethora of workers to choose from. A young registered nurse started work in a small clinic in an average size town. As she gained experience and skills she moved up her career ladder until she was offered a head nurse appointment in a large medical center. Her dilemma was that she had topped out of her profession both in prestige and financial enumeration at her present setting. If she relocates to the larger city, she leaves trusted friends and family who are a daily part of her life. Her lifestyle would change drastically as everything would be different. It's a trade-off but an important decision that only she can make.

Small towns do give you a certain intimacy; the grocery clerks know you but that intimacy can also mean a lack of privacy. The entire town knows when you get a new car, or paint your back fence. They know you love the Steelers and give really good Christmas parties. And they know when you and your significant other break up (and why), that you're struggling to meet your bills, and that your cousin is pregnant.

When I first started teaching, I lived in the small town where I taught at the local junior high school. When I was at the grocery store, students would approach me, and see that I had something like beer in my shopping cart. They were amazed that one of their teachers drank beer! And that they liked the same kind of cereal I did. For some, this closeness and intimacy is comforting; for me, it felt more like an intrusion into my private life. This is why so many teachers and police officers do not live in the town where they work. Would this bother you? It is something to think about.

Midsize towns are the same as small towns, but the familiarity aspect takes longer to establish. After three or four years most of the town's population know the inside information on everyone, too.

Large towns or major cities give you a certain amount of anonymity because of the increase in population. Going to the hardware store in old baggy pants will not get you banned from the well-dressed club because no one cares. There is, of course, more traffic and higher costs of living, but there are also museums, cultural events, major league sports, and more.

Luciano Mortula/Shutterstock, Inc.

Where you live affects the bottom line of your paycheck. Can you afford to take that entry-level position in San Francisco where an apartment can cost several thousand dollars a month? A teacher friend of mine commutes 45 minutes a day each way to teach in the Bay area. His salary will not cover living closer to his work. Jan and Melissa share an apartment in Berkeley, California, and still pay almost 50% of their take-home dollars for housing. Food is also expensive, especially fresh fruit and vegetables. They say they're having a wonderful time exploring and experimenting, however.

It's like that old Spanish proverb, "Take what you want. Take what you want and pay for it."

Spare time and hobbies

No one works all the time so what do you do with the rest of the hours in a day? What are your favorite things to do with your excess energy? Where you choose to live will affect your hobbies. Don't believe me? Try parasailing in Alaska. Are you an outdoors kind of person or is your idea of a good vacation a book with a beach attached? Are you a traveler or a stay-at-home garden sitter? By the time you are of an age and position to seek gainful employment, you have discovered some likes and a host of dislikes on how you spend your free time. Some of those pros and cons will affect where you want to settle. The nightlife of Seattle is not the nightlife of Kingsburg, California (a town of about 10,000 in the Central Valley, mostly agricultural). The basic community of small-town Kingsburg cannot be duplicated in big-city Seattle. See, no right or wrong; depends on individual desires and personal requirements.

There are a host of hobbies that can be practiced anywhere: reading, woodcraft, hiking, bicycling, etc. Paul took a so-so job in order to be close to the ocean to surf as much as he wanted. He discovered that "as much as he wanted" was very little. A vacation hobby wasn't fun when done all the time. He has since taken a better job in Arizona.

RESEARCH

What all this means is you need to get on your computer and do some research. Each city or town has a website that provides all the demographics of the area. Check out the medium income, the housing/rental market, the population and its projected growth. What are the main points of interest in the area? What do people do for fun? Are there good hospitals and specialists in the area if you have the need for them? Is the area someplace where you want to live 12 months a year? Does the weather satisfy you? Living in Wisconsin means snow, lots of snow. Living in a beach city means lots of summer tourists. Will that be a major problem for you? There are two ways to find out. The first is to do lots of research using all the resources you can find (including the library). The second is to spend your vacation or at least a week in the area where you are interested in moving. Again, if you do move and hate the new job, the road travels both ways.

Other things to consider

Ask yourself: "What don't I do well?" Right away *my* mind shifts to the mechanics of handwriting. Everything in my life is on a computer. I have dysgraphia, which means that I have a disorder that makes my handwriting difficult to read. (My teachers just said my handwriting was poor or that I was lazy.) Anything that requires handwriting will not be my chosen profession. Maybe yours is algebraic equations, or engine repair, or a host of other things. The important thing is not what you can or can't do, but recognizing your strengths and weaknesses.

Sometimes even the things you do really well hold little interest for you. Bryan is an accomplished artist but doing it every day bores him silly. Remember that word *compromise*. Brian could have decided to teach in one of the creative fields. Instead he chose to partner with his father in a jewelry store, a creative outlet for him. A cousin is a hot shot in dealing with money but he actively dislikes working with finances; instead he chose to become a pediatric nurse which he says satisfies his need to nurture.

The point is you, and only you, make the ***"happy"*** decision. You, and only you, decide if the job is right for you. Whether it's as a social worker in a group home or dipping ice cream in a sandwich shop, only you decide.

AVOID RASH DECISIONS

Some decisions we all make are based on uncertain factors, at best. Kathy H. had to declare a college major. She likes kids, she wanted to work inside, and she hates to get really dirty, so Kathy decided that teaching would be a good profession for her because it was projected by her college that teachers would be needed within a five-year period. She felt set; unfortunately an economic recession occurred where older teachers didn't retire and school finances were tight. No decision on job training should ever be based on what you (or others) think will be hirable.

During a major expansion of internet companies, Joe S. went to work for a start-up computer company that paid well. His job was to input and analyze computer data amassed from internet sources.

He found that he was good at the job but absolutely hated to go to work every morning. After much angst, he quit. If it's not for you, move on to something that is. Joe now works for an in-home computer repair service; he likes the computer work but not the lack of people interaction.

Mandy A. has always wanted to work in the medical field as a service provider. When she got engaged to her high school sweetheart, she had to rethink some priorities. A physician takes years of training, a nurse or physician's assistant would take less time and could be attained locally. Sometimes a trade-off in time, training, money, as well as ultimate responsibilities, has to be considered.

A cousin (and yes, I have a ton of cousins) just gave up a potentially lucrative career in the business world to go back to school to train to be a school psychologist. Another cousin decided that college was not for him and became an auto mechanic specializing in foreign custom cars. He makes more money than any of us and loves his work.

There's no such thing as being stuck in a job. Just like you can move from a city, you can move into a different career. And not all careers, or all people, require a college education. Training is usually essential—we really aren't born knowing much—but where and how we get the training is up for grabs.

A t-shirt worn by a group of swimmers said:

IF IT'S TO BE IT'S UP TO ME

That says it all.

DISCUSSION QUESTIONS

1. How much time should you spend each day looking for a job?
2. Why is attitude so important in the job market?
3. What kinds of things belong in your "I'm Awesome" folder? What is the purpose of creating this folder, anyway?
4. Give an example of the difference between arrogance and confidence.
5. What are companies looking for?
6. What are soft skills?

TERMS TO REMEMBER

Soft skills	Social media	Interviews
Awesome	Networking	Cover letter

THINGS TO REMEMBER

- Attitude will make you or break you.
- Looking for a job is a real job.
- Research companies to become knowledgeable of their goals.
- Creating an "I'm Awesome" folder pulls the positives together.

REFERENCES

Ackerman, J. M., and J. A. Bargh. (2010). The purpose-driven life: Commentary on Kenrick et al. *Perspectives on Psychological Science*, 5, 323-326.

Maslow, Abraham. (1943). Retrieved November 15, 2014, from http://www.simplypsychology.org/maslow.html

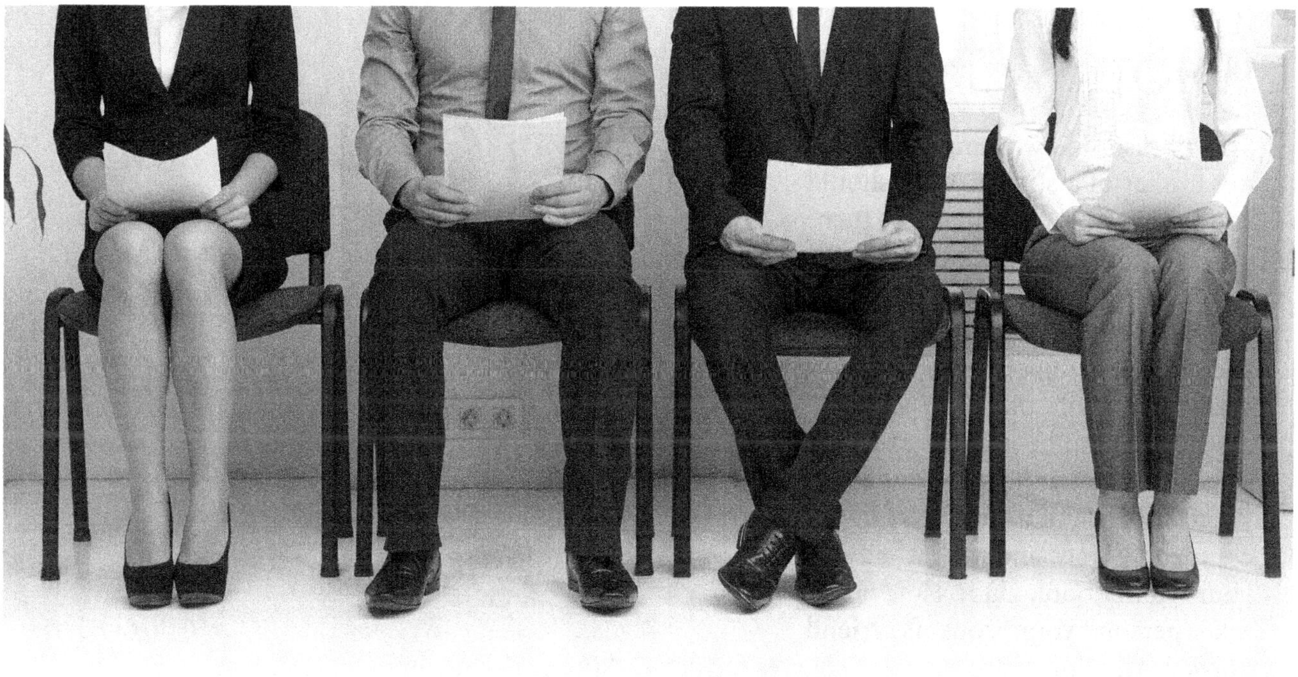

CHAPTER 3

NETWORKING:
The What, Who, Where, How, and When

You're at the point of actively looking for work. No one has come to beat on your door requesting you to work for them at some astronomical salary. Now you have to start actively looking for work. You need to network and talk to people about a job.

WHAT

Networking is defined as follows:
network, 'net-wərk/ verb

- gerund or present participle: networking
- to connect as or operate with a network
- "The stock exchanges have proven to be resourceful in *networking* these deals."
- to link (machines, especially computers) to operate interactively
- "*networked* workstations"
- to interact with other people to exchange information and develop contacts, especially to further one's career
- "the skills of *networking*, bargaining, and negotiation"

WHO

Andresr/Shutterstock, Inc.

The phrase "networking is life" is not too far of a stretch. Who should you network with? Well, it turns out literally everyone you meet is an opportunity to network. Many people do not realize that all of their friends, the people in their classes/workplace, their places of worship, and their family are all excellent sources of networking. How about your Dad's friend who works for that company? How about that lady in your Mom's book club? How about that person your cousin's friend knows? All of these are excellent sources for networking to assist you in your career.

Don't forget your old friends from school. They are doing something to earn a living. Your Facebook friends (and their Facebook friends) are a great source for getting your message out there. Ask for advice on where to go next in your job search. Some people have literally hundreds of Facebook friends; I think my niece has 900. All those readers know other people. Don't be shy—ask for their advice and take it. Then send an e-mail to thank them for their help.

WHERE

You look everywhere when on a quest for a job. Yes, you look in your chosen field but you also want to branch out. If you want a job in marketing, for instance, you check out large companies that have advertising departments. If you want a job as an administrative assistant, then you think outside the box and apply at school offices besides the regular professional offices. Jill M. graduated college as a social worker but after four months of seriously applying everywhere she could think of, she was stymied. A friend suggested applying at non-profit agencies. She was hired by a non-profit working with foster children; a perfect fit for Jill, allowing her to use her education and help children. Another option she could have tried was working in city or state government.

Most people only want to apply for jobs that are advertised and where there is a "now hiring" sign. Unfortunately, most jobs are not advertised, or only by word of mouth. That's why networking is so important. If your finances allow, applying in your selected field makes sense. That is the fast track to move up in your career. If money is needed now to pay the rent, you take whatever job is available and still continue your career job search. You go from store to store in the mall, talking to people and applying at small business and large ones, too. **Needs must trump desires in some cases.**

HOW

Igor Zakowski/Shutterstock, Inc.

So, how do we do it? How do we network? Is it just a way of talking to people? Aren't we going to annoy the heck out of people?

Well, first we need to know what to say to people. My advice is this: Don't ask them for a job. Wait, what? You say, how am I going to do it if I don't talk to them about a job? Let's ask some basic psychological questions: Do you like to say no to people? How do you feel when you do? I know when I have to say no to someone, I feel bad. Consequently, the next time I see that person, I am going to be reminded of this fact. "Oh dang, here comes so and so, and last time I talked to him, I had to turn him down, so maybe I'll just avoid him."

Now, let's turn it the other way. How do you feel when someone says, "You're an expert!" or "You know so much about people!" That validates us and makes us feel good. We all have a little bit of an ego and having that ego stroked is nice. So, what about if instead of asking them for a job, we ask them for some career advice? With advice, I don't have to say no to you, and I feel good, after all, you felt that I was so smart I could help you. A win-win. So let's say the initial conversation goes something like this:

Job seeker: Hey I haven't seen you in a while, how have you and your family been?
Expert: We've been good, what have you been up to?
Job seeker: I'm just graduating from college in (inset your major/career goal here) *or* My company is moving out of state and I'm needed here for my parents.
Expert: (to self) Oh no, I hope he/she doesn't ask me for a job, we don't have any openings at my business.
Job seeker: I'm glad I ran into you, you have always been kind of a mentor to me and always helpful; do you have any advice for me in my career search?
Expert: (to self) Wow, he thinks of me as a mentor, that's pretty cool, hmmm.
Expert: Yeah, I remember that you are good at such and so; give me a day or so to do some checking. Do you have your contact information?
Job seeker: Yes, here is my card. I'll call you next week if that would be OK.
Expert: Absolutely, I'm glad to help.

See how easy that is? You did not embarrass the "expert." You made the person feel good, and maybe got some free advice. Even if your experts don't have anything, they may know of someone else they could call and that contact could help. Or they may think of someone later. Nothing but a few minutes is lost. Some folks may not be helpful and your advice asking may go askew but the main thing is that you are out there trying. And just like anything else, each time gets easier. Honest.

"Oh, but that's embarrassing to walk up to someone and ask for suggestions." To quote one of my favorite TV shows, *Deadliest Catch*, "Suck it up, Buttercup." Finding employment is not easy. No one is going to come running up to you and say, "Oh pretty please, let me hire you!" You have an arduous process ahead of you and you better believe you need all the allies you can get in your corner.

WHEN

Antonio Guillem/Shutterstock, Inc.

The when is very simple—it's until you find a job. As was stated in the first chapter, you treat getting a job like a job. You get up, get dressed, eat breakfast, and look for work. You take an hour break for lunch and then you're back at it until 5 p.m. *Six* days a week! This is serious business. If you sleep until 10 a.m., surf the television until after lunch, and promise yourself you'll buckle down after the highlights of the football game are over, furget-bout-it. With ZERO motivation that's what you're going to get, ZERO. No business, store, company, or individual is going to your door begging you to take a job offer. There's a surplus of potential employees for a finite number of jobs. Getting a job is not hopeless, but major effort *is* required.

Make a list of the companies in your field that you would like to work for. Check their websites to see if they are hiring, even if their employment offerings is in a related field to what you want. Get an application and apply. Then call the manager and discuss your options. Tell the manager you just applied online but would like to meet face to face as you want to ask advice about how to best start in this field. Tell the manager why you want to work for this company. (This means you need to have all those interview skills in the upcoming interview chapters.) Keep track of who you have called and the contact's name with a short self-reminder of the gist of the conversation. (How about making a document with this information and putting it into your "I'm Awesome" folder?)

It is estimated only 20% of jobs are gained through the internet (*WSJ*, 2014). Most of the time, a friend of a friend knows someone who he or she would like to work with and recommends this person for an upcoming job that will never be advertised. One of my nephews worked for a pizza company that ONLY hired from referrals. The owner said that his employees knew the people they were vouching for and did a better job of hiring than his one-time interview ever did. His turnover was close to zero.

Scope out the physical plant or building of the company. Dress appropriately as if it was an interview because it may end up as one. If it's a large company, check with human resources (HR, or some call it Personnel), introduce yourself, and let them know that you have applied and sent in your resume. Talk to them about your goals and again how you want to work for their particular company. Be prepared to answer question for both standard and behavioral interviews. If it's a small place, ask to speak to the owner or manager to talk about how it would be best in applying to such a company. Explain that you are looking for a job and provide a short synopsis of your skills and experience—akin to your elevator pitch. This is also the answer, by the way, to the first interview question most people ask, "Tell me about yourself."

Remember me mentioning the "elevator pitch"—that short (two- or three-minute) talk about you? It goes like this: My name is Joe (or Jenny) Jobseeker and I just graduated with a degree in _______ from _____________. I majored in this because I really enjoy working with people and it fits my personality. I am especially interested in your company because you work with __________ and that has long been an interest of mine. I also enjoy working and building _________ in my spare time and I think all of these attributes make me an ideal candidate for working with the people and infrastructure in your company.

See, short and to the point; what you can say between the bottom and top floor riding in an elevator. If they want more, let them ask you about it. Here is a link to an excellent video on how to answer this: https://www.youtube.com/watch?v=-ezFNrWMTlc

VOLUNTEERING

If at all possible, volunteer in a field similar to your career path. Start as soon as possible. It looks really good on your resume besides giving you some personal experiences in the field and potentially a huge source of people for networking. If you want to be a nurse and you've volunteered at the local hospital, the administrative powers-that-be know you have some idea of the field. A friend thought she wanted to be a preschool teacher because she loved taking care of the church nursery. She volunteered in a local preschool and she was right; it fit her personality perfectly. (It could have easily gone the other way.) Manny G. had worked for his dad running a fertilizer plant since he was young. He, and his dad, assumed that he would one day take over the business. While study Ag Business in college he volunteered to help a very cute girl with her horticultural project and fell in love—not with the girl but with the field. Thankfully Joe's dad backed his son's choices. Plans do change as we gain more knowledge.

No time? BS! An hour a day or two hours a week of volunteer work broadens your scope of networking. (Evenings are wonderful times to volunteer at homeless shelters where the need is always great for servers, and helpers.) People know other people and if they are impressed with your skills and attitude most are willing to help further your goals. One teacher told me that everyone she helps, in her regular school day or as special cases, a little bit of <u>her</u> is passed on. Same thing; volunteering will open other doors for you.

If college is your thing, most programs insist on an internship or work in your field—with credit attached. Those internships are invaluable as they offer you experience in the workplace of your choice. The teacher/professor has built his or her own networking system to help students further their goals. Again, student success is also teacher success.

Any, and I do mean *any*, volunteer work is better than none. Painting a neighbor's house with the church group doesn't look on paper like a valuable asset but it shows a potential employer your compassion, work ethic, and integrity. Refereeing for a little league baseball team might be fun but it also shows that you care for your community and are committed to the development of young people. If you really can't find a place to volunteer with your limited amount of time, call your county volunteer office. They beg for people to teach basic reading to individuals (no training required), help serve meals at senior centers, and meet a multitude of other unfilled needs. And there are a ton of those in today's economy. It always amazes me that even schools have finally caught on that volunteering helps develop students' commitments and values, and creates better academic students. Most high schools now require a certain number of unpaid community service hours to graduate, too.

Back to the basic networking premise: Network with everyone. Everyone is a source in looking for help in getting a job. And remember, an enthusiastic, friendly attitude goes a long way when it comes to referrals for employment, as does a "thank you" along the way.

ORGANIZATIONS

These associations will probably be one of your best resources. Here you will find people already employed in your chosen field, who are usually the movers and shakers in the area. Different organizations draw different kinds of people (for example, small-town Rotary Clubs and Ag Groups). Pretty self-explanatory but this intermingling of like-minded people is conducive to networking at its best. Young blood is always needed to keep the groups going. An enthusiastic new person with a friendly attitude will be a welcome addition.

One person found his dream job this way. He had just graduated from Cal Poly, San Luis Obispo with a degree in Agricultural Business. He noticed all of the "old-timers" hung out at the local donut shop for coffee early in the morning. He knew a couple of them and asked if he could sit with them one morning. He kept quiet for a while until they had accepted his presence. He learned all kinds of things! These people knew everything that went on not only in their town, but pretty much the whole county! (Old-timers all know and talk to each other!) One morning after he had been there for a while, one of them asked what field of work he was in. The old-timer said, "Hmmmm" and that was it. Two days later, the same old-timer said, "Son, let me introduce you to so and so, he runs a bunch of ranches in this area." Long story short, the guy he was introduced to retired, and he now runs all those ranches. Sometimes you have to get creative to get the job done!

Before you go to the meeting check to see if there are any names you recognize and try to talk to them at the meeting. At the meeting ask for a list of members. That might not be available to you but a list of the officers of the group will be (probably also online). At the minimum, set up an appointment to ask for advice (first part of this chapter). If the group is volunteering for anything—toys for tots, roadside cleanup, or anything else—volunteer to help with the project. This will allow for further conversations and they will understand both your sincerity and your work ethic.

Blend Images/Shutterstock, Inc.

One young lady said that she couldn't possibly just walk into a meeting uninvited. Hello! That's what networking is all about—getting a job preferably in your career sphere. Men and women join these organizations so they can be with others with the same areas of interest and that does mean you, too. This is also a good place to look for a person who would be willing and able to mentor a neophyte. A mentor is an advisor and coach. Most people want to pass on their wisdom and knowledge: mentoring is a win-win for both sides. There might be someone in the organization who likes to mentor deserving individuals and the young woman might be just the one she is looking for.

Don't forget the local unemployment agencies, both government run and private. The state agency is a good resource for leads. Oftentimes the job listings at the state unemployment agency are at entry level, but this gives you a foot in the door, so to speak. Private employment agencies usually charge the employer a fee, not the person seeking employment. Personally, I held a managerial position in retail for two years which I obtained through a private employment outfit. I kept that job while I went back to school part time.

TEMPORARY EMPLOYMENT AGENCIES

Temp agencies are often a life saver. "Forget about my dream job, I need to pay the rent and eat until something else turns up." This puts a whole different spin on your game plan. You take whatever jobs come along and more power to you, usually minimum wage and short-term positions. Remember to let the temp agency know that you have a multitude of skills and are seeking employment in such and such. Ask for those jobs that are peripheral to your own goals. When you go to a new temporary workplace make sure you do an outstanding job and continue to network with other employees.

Temporary employment is often another of those win-wins. You get to be paid while working—hopefully in your wanted realm of employment. Temp hires are just that—putting an individual in a workplace where an employer needs help for a short time period. Temp hires could be from one day to several months depending on the particular employer situation. As a temporary employee you may be able to work in several places over a period of several weeks. Each new workplace gives you an opportunity to network with a new group of people. Many temporary positions also turn into permanent positions if the temp hire works well within the office team.

Remember that temp work is a real job. It may not be a forever job but most entry level jobs seldom are. (Most people change jobs every few years.) You need to dress appropriately for each job site, and follow the rules of interviewing; be on time and never talk negatively about an employer (even if the person is a jerk). Never – ever! Make each job site a successful performance so that at the end of your hire the temporary employer will consent to writing you a glowing referral.

FOLLOW-UP

Hywit Dimyadi/Shutterstock, Inc.

Become organized. Keep track of people who have helped you and either send a thank you e-mail or a personal note. (You'll need thank-you notes anyway after any interview. The local dollar store is a nice place to buy them.)

Thank-you notes do several things. First, they make you stand out from the normal crowd—very few people take the time to send thank-you notes anymore. Secondly, because of the first reason, whoever receives one will think of you in positive terms. And third, it's a classy gesture. It speaks that your mama did a good job; you have manners and are appreciative of the help given.

RESEARCH

Researching companies is essential! Notice the exclamation mark? Absolutely essential. You wouldn't walk into a store to see what they are selling, so do not make the same mistake with companies/businesses you want to work with. Think of the business as a large company like Macys. What different departments are there? What does each department sell—clothing, dishes, or shoes? Same thing when you research a company. What do they sell or what service do they provide? Who owns the company? What are its goals? In retail it's easier; they want to provide materials for people to buy so they can make a profit. The service industry is harder only because profit and service co-exist. You need to think as if you were doing the hiring. What questions would you ask if someone talked to you?

Now to your most important questions of all: "What can I offer this company? What will they see in me that they hire me instead of other applicants?" With each company you research as a potential employee, ask yourself "What can I bring to the table? Experience? Enthusiasm? Good looks? Great customer skills?" Each company will have very different needs: the perfume salesperson at Macy's will require different skill sets than a receptionist at a stockyard or a data processing clerk. The more you are prepared the more people will recognize your ability and help you with finding employment.

You absolutely must know basic facts about the company and preferably what the company's goals are so that you can prioritize your skills to best fit the company's jobs. Use the internet and examine the backgrounds of people you want to talk with. (The internet is not the best site to find employment but it is the best place to find information.) Again check to see if you know anyone working for the company for a possible referral.

Generally speaking, I can't stress enough that:
1. Networking is talking to everyone in the right way.
2. Looking for work is a 24/7 job—you're always "on stage."
3. It's up to you to join organizations preferably in your chosen field.
4. Volunteering shows initiative and a strong work ethic.
5. Thank-you notes and e-mails are classy.
6. Research proves to the potential employer that you are interested in the business.

DISCUSSION QUESTIONS

1. What do you need to say in an elevator pitch? Write it out.
2. Who do you network with and how do you do it best?
3. Give two examples of how an organization could be of help to you in your job search. How would you initiate that?
4. Why would a thank-you note be important in the business world?
5. Name three ways to gain experience in your job search. Which would be best for you personally?

TERMS TO REMEMBER

Elevator pitch	Mentors	Advising
Volunteering	Referrals	Organizations

THINGS TO REMEMBER

- Network with literally everyone.
- Ask for advice, not a job.
- Network until you have a job.
- Treat finding a job as a six-day, 8-to-5 job.

REFERENCE

Krueger, K. R., and B. Moore. (2015). New technology "clouds" student data privacy. *Phi Delta Kappan, 96*(5), 19. doi:10.1177/0031721715569464

Smith, J. (2013, April 16). How social media can help (or hurt) your job search. Retrieved November 16, 2014, from http://www.forbes.com/sites/jacquelynsmith/2013/04/16/how-social-media-can-help-or-hurt-your-job-search/

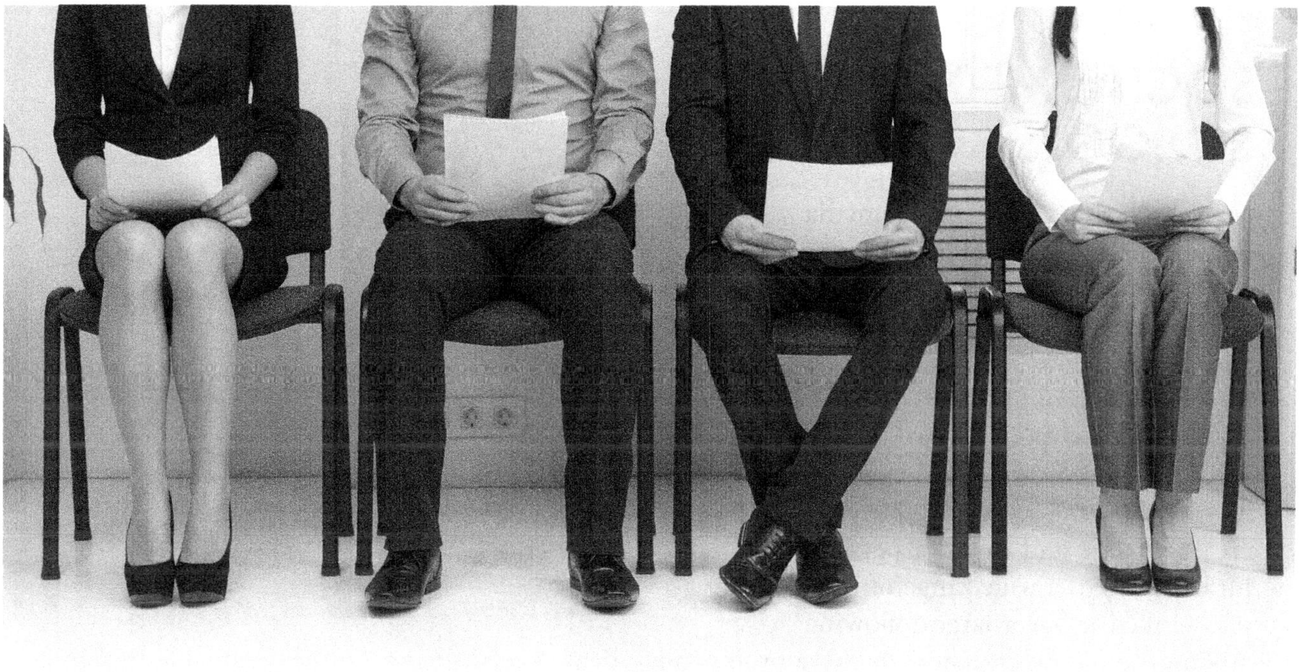

CHAPTER 4

SOCIAL MEDIA AND YOUR JOB CAMPAIGN

Nowadays, social media is everywhere, from your home computer to sports teams to your favorite products wanting you to "like" them on their Facebook page; we are literally surrounded with it. For our purposes, we need to see how to effectively use this medium in our searches.

First, what is social media for? It is good for getting your message out and, as the Networking chapter explained, for expanding and reaching a wide variety of people in a short space of time. When you post something, say on Facebook, you are (depending on your privacy settings) posting not only to your friends and family, but also to all of their friends and family, like that small pebble dropped in the pond creating ever-expanding circles. This allows your friends and their friends and their friend's friends to help you, not only in your search for employment but for mentoring, social outlets, and a host of other endeavors. From online romance to class reunions, Facebook has become vital.

SOCIAL MEDIA IN SCHOOLS

Oleksiy Mark/Shutterstock, Inc.

Many schools are using social media in their classes, including such things as Facebook, Twitter, and YouTube videos to increase their knowledge base; some allow students to check their e-mail accounts, or go on Facebook as a classroom reward. Social media has become a force on many high school and college campuses to create change and to get a person's ideas across to a wide range of people. LinkedIn has a large following among the nation's teachers to share professional ideas. Social media can be a valuable tool in a variety of ways. Technology is part of our daily lives and will become a bigger and bigger issue in the future.

Privacy Caution

An issue of privacy in all aspects of technology is becoming a major source of worry for all of us. From your credit card identification to information collected by businesses to government databases, we are all at risk of having what we consider "my business" stolen. This stolen info can be sold, posted online, or used for purposes other than our own intentions.

Hackers are oftentimes from other countries where laws cannot touch them or even garner information to catch them. And these hackers are smart, really smart. They create fake websites that resemble the ones we are familiar with, they phone with information from a well-known company insisting they need to update your computer, and on and on. Each new day brings another new scam.

Schools with student data have been a source of data hacking for several years to gain information for direct advertising to the student or for more unsavory purposes. The basic concern for school systems is that all information should stay local under the control of the school itself for the protection of the student, the parents, and the school.

First, and I say this several times in other chapters: **Do Not Put Anything on the Internet That You Do Not Want Published to the World,** because it could be. There is no such thing as deleting something permanently on a hard drive or on the internet for a professional hacker. The only way to protect yourself in this day is to secure your devices, have strong passwords changed often, and regularly review your accounts. Oh, and watch your internet usage in Wi-Fi places, especially while traveling.

Cyberbullying

Unfortunately, social media in schools have also impacted in another negative way—that is, bullying has a new platform and has far lasting results. Cyberbullying is using technology to intimidate, insult, or harass (Witsoe, 2012). Cyberbullying has become such a prevalent factor in the news that the president of the United States has recognized the problem area.

As a friend's middle school daughter told me, "Kids do it because you can fight and be mean online. It's easy and it makes you not afraid." This from a normal, good kid. She went on to say that lots of her friends spread untrue rumors either online or by texting about other people that they don't like. By high school, students are usually more apt with computer usage and can hide behind a false name and e-mail more readily. I hope they have a little more maturity and compassion.

Most of young people's time is spent at school. Most cyberbullying is done on weekends and at night, not during school hours. Schools have the dilemma of whether to get involved, as it does impact the learning environment. There is not a consistent policy, although more and more schools are becoming aware that cyberbullying is more widespread with sometimes deadly effects for the vulnerable student. Some schools retain a "hands-off policy" since the activity takes place in the privacy of the student's home. Others are trying to negotiate a middle ground with parent conferences and student workshops. From judges to principals to parents, everyone has an opinion as to what needs to be done. What they all realize is that technology is here to stay and its consequences cannot be ignored or negative impacts tolerated.

For me, the biggest problem is that the most defenseless among us is usually the one who is a target for the aggressive, immature kids lashing out from their own personal issues. According to Scholastic.com, 42% of kids have been bullied online; one in four have had it happen more than once. Their research says that 58% of kids have received mean or threatening e-mails or other messages; 14% have not told their parents about the online bullying incident. Their parents did not grow up with technology as they have and the next generation will be even more steeped in it. Rules, knowledge, and maybe even some laws will have be implemented to protect the safety of children and maybe even adults.

Does cyberbullying or bullying happen in the workplace? Cyberbullying almost never. Bullying yes, but not so much and it is usually more subtle. Most adult computer users recognize that the internet is a permanent storage compartment and it's easy to get caught making untrue statements. Bullying in the workplace is a deviant behavior trait and hopefully that employee does not last long. For most employers, anyone who can't work successfully as a team member is gone. Period. Petty and not-so-petty problems that spill over into work are verboten and must be solved or left at home. The bottom line is the company product, its goals and services.

Any person looking for employment needs to know that whatever you post on Facebook, Twitter, e-mails, iPhone, etc., can all be accessed by a computer geek. **Do Not Ever Say Anything on the Net You Don't Want Out There.**

Here is a website on college students and social media: http://blog.tunheim.com/2012/03/09/how-college-students-use-social-media/129#.VQL4JfzF-E4 It explains how college students use social media; it also lets you know that many professors also use social media, some of them in their classes (the horror, adults using social media).

TERMS YOU NEED TO KNOW

INSTANT MESSAGING - Instant messaging (IM) is a form of real-time, direct text-based communication between two or more people. More advanced instant messaging software clients also allow enhanced modes of communication, such as live voice or video calling.

KLOUT - Klout is a measure of social influence. The service allows users to connect various social accounts such as Facebook, Flickr, YouTube, etc., and then provides every user with a personal Klout score. The score is out of 100—the higher the score, the more influence you have on the social world.

LIKE - A "Like" is an action that can be made by a Facebook user. Instead of writing a comment for a message or a status update, a Facebook user can click the "Like" button as a quick way to show approval and share the message.

LINKEDIN - LinkedIn is a business-oriented social networking site. Founded in December 2002 and launched in May 2003, it is mainly used for professional networking. As of June 2010, LinkedIn had more than 70 million registered users, spanning more than 200 countries and territories worldwide.

LURKER - A lurker online is a person who reads discussions on a message board, newsgroup, social network, or other interactive system, but rarely or never participates in the discussion.

MEME - A meme on the internet is used to describe a thought, idea, joke, or concept to be shared online. It is typically an image with text above and below it, but can also come in video and link form. A popular example is the "I Can Has Cheezburger?" cat meme that turned into an entire site of memes.

MYSPACE - MySpace is a social networking website owned by News Corporation. MySpace became the most popular social networking site in the United States in June 2006 and was overtaken internationally by its main competitor, Facebook, in April 2008.

NEWS FEED - A news feed is literally a feed full of news. On Facebook, the News Feed is the homepage of users' accounts where they can see all the latest updates from their friends. The news feed on Twitter is called Timeline (not to get confused with Facebook's new look, also called Timeline).

PANDORA - Pandora is a social online radio station that allows users to create stations based on their favorite artists and types of music.

PLATFORM - a platform refers to the type of social media being used. This includes Facebook, YouTube, Twitter, and Instagram.

PODCAST - A podcast, or non-streamed webcast, is a series of digital media files, either audio or video, that are released episodically and often downloaded through an RSS feed.

POST - A post is the process of placing content on a social media network.

REDDIT - Reddit is similar to Digg. It is a social news site that is built upon a community of users who share and comment on stories.

RETWEET - A retweet is when someone on Twitter sees your message and decides to re-share it with his/her followers. A retweet button allows them to quickly resend the message with attribution to the original sharer's name.

RSS FEED - RSS (Really Simple Syndication) is a family of web feed formats used to publish frequently updated content such as blogs and videos in a standardized format. Content publishers can syndicate a feed, which allows users to subscribe to the content and read it when they please, and from a location other than the website (such as reader services like Google Reader).

SEARCH ENGINE OPTIMIZATION - Search engine optimization is the process of improving the volume or quality of traffic to a website from search engines via unpaid or organic search traffic.

SKYPE - Skype is a free program that allows for text, audio, and video chats between users.

SOCIAL MEDIA - Social media is media designed to be disseminated through social interaction, created using highly accessible and scalable publishing techniques.

YOUTUBE - A video sharing site owned by Google. Users can freely upload their own video content to the site. YouTube makes it easy for people to embed videos on their own site or blogs, which helps with viral marketing efforts.

HOW TO USE SOCIAL MEDIA

For me, I use Facebook to keep track of all my friends and family from all over the country and even the world. I don't use it to post recipes or to take a picture of what I had for dinner. Some of my friends are political and post various memes and statements about one side of the political spectrum or another. I try to look at them with an open mind, but it is hard sometimes.

Now, one of the facts of our modern times, you can actually get a job as a social media director for a company! This position did not exist even a few short years ago. For the university where I work, our social media director works closely with marketing and public relations to keep a positive image for the university. Why am I mentioning this? Well, there are also people who get hired to check on what people are saying about their company on social media. These networks are becoming increasingly powerful and can have a real impact on a company's cash flow and profits.

HOW EMPLOYERS USE SOCIAL MEDIA

So what does this have to do with you? These same companies are now checking on potential and present employees' social media accounts. Many of them are now checking on social media accounts to help screen potential applicants. For example, "Greg Simpson, a senior vice president at Lee Hecht Harrison, said in a press statement that job seekers must understand how hiring managers and recruiters are using social media in all phases of the selection process."

To help job seekers better understand the role of social media in their job search, CareerBuilder.com conducted a survey last year that asked 2,303 hiring managers and human resource professionals if, how, and why they incorporate social media into their hiring process. First, they found that 37% of employers use social networks to screen potential job candidates. That means about two in five companies browse your social media profiles to evaluate your character and personality—and some even base their hiring decision on what they find.

"Social media is a primary vehicle of communication today, and because much of that communication is public, it's no surprise some recruiters and hiring managers are tuning in," says Rosemary Haefner, vice president of human resources at CareerBuilder. CareerBuilder also asked employers why they use social networks to research candidates, and 65% said they do it to see if the job seeker presents himself or herself professionally. About half (51%) want to know if the candidate is a good fit for the company culture, and another 45% want to learn more about his or her qualifications. Some cited "to see if the candidate is well-rounded" and "to look for reasons not to hire the candidate," as their motives.

Too many red cups

So, how do we deal with this? Let me respond with a true story from my brother-in-law. It's called "Too Many Red Cups." My brother-in-law was flying from Los Angeles to Salt Lake City a few years ago. He found himself sitting next to a nicely dressed young man in the window seat muttering to himself. Once they were in the air, my brother-in-law (we'll call him Joe) asked the young man what was wrong, and the young man said, "Too many red cups!" Well, he then asked him what that meant, so the young man (we'll call him Alex) told him this story: "I was in LA for a third and final interview for a major Fortune 500 company. The hiring came down to me and another person so they flew us to the company headquarters. We spent the day doing things like several face-to-face interviews, with everyone from the immediate supervisor to the company CEO. We also did those stupid personality tests; you know the kind where they ask you a hundred questions and the third and the ninety-seventh one are the same to see if you answer similar? Well, I did fine on those, so did the other candidate. The company checked our GPAs, both were very high. So, finally I guess the company checked our social media profiles, now neither of us were saints, we both had a normal time in college. Studied a lot, went to a few parties. The difference was, I had posted pictures from a few of those parties with me having a good time. I thought my privacy settings were good but it turns out mine were fine but some of my friend's privacy settings were not. Anyway, they saw those pictures of me having a good time. In several of them, I had one of those red Solo cups in my hand (made infamous by the Toby Keith song). Apparently, the other candidate didn't post pictures like that or had taken them down. Long story short, he got the job and I didn't because of those stupid red Solo cups!" Upon relating this story to my niece, she immediately went to her social media sites and took down a bunch of pictures; she won't tell us which ones. So, that is how it can affect you!

LINKEDIN

Next, let's look at another website, LinkedIn. I will tell this story through the video of a friend of mine, J. Vincent Nix. He was a colleague of mine and is now an administrator in a community college in Montana. He took a course on how to use this site and I will pass it on to you.

What follows is a synopsis of his visiting speaker role in one of my classes. Vince says (with a little bit of my own stuff thrown in): What I'm talking about today is LinkedIn but I'm going to give you a little bit of a foundation on networking because that's what's necessary. Let me tell you what LinkedIn is—LinkedIn is not a social media site, it is a career networking web tool. It is just one of many tools you can use when you graduate and start your career search. You don't just want a job, you want a career. A job is a step in a career. You'll have a series of jobs in your career. How many of you already have a LinkedIn profile created? For those of you who have not, consider creating a profile. When you're thinking about putting something on LinkedIn or any social media site, consider this, "Would I want my grandmother to see this?" If the answer is no, it doesn't belong online anywhere during your career search. The reason I say this is there are some companies that are requiring us to show them our social media profiles. When Vince decided to come back to the United States (he spent six years teaching in China), he had to redo his profiles (Facebook and other social media sites are blocked in China). When you start setting up your profile, you need to focus on what you are putting online.

Profiles

I use four key messages in my profile on LinkedIn. They are a career summary, an exit statement, a value proposition, and relocation. Before you set up your profile, think about what kind of statement you want to make. This should be in succinct, one- or two-sentence statements. This is not the same as the objective on a resume. Think of the headline in a newspaper or your favorite online news source, now think about what you want the headline for your job search to be. How do you want to catch people's attention? Your headline should be about you!

Career summary

Your short career summary should cover what you have been doing for the last few years. Many of you will have been in school, some of you will be older and will be going back to school. (Both Vince and I started school at age 26; we are both still taking classes, and I doubt if I will ever stop.) So the question is how you are going to parlay that experience into future job opportunities. Think of your headline and now think of your theme. This is what goes on your career summary.

Exit statement

Your exit statement explains why you left your last job or career. For most people reading this book, that is fairly easy. You left your last job or position to go to school. However, once you have a job, and leave it to go to another one, you need to be able to communicate why you left without communicating that you were upset about something and that's why you left. Sometimes we get laid off. If you say, "I left my last job because those *#@*&^%$ laid me off," it is not going to go over well. You might say something like, "they streamlined the organization" or "my supervisor and I thought it would be best if I left the organization to pursue other opportunities." NEVER badmouth a previous employer, no matter what.

Value proposition

Your value proposition is what makes you stand out from everyone else. What makes you unique? In other words, what makes you so hireable? We are not talking about the fact you have a cool car or truck or that you can tie a cherry stem in a knot with your tongue. We are talking about relevant skills that will show up in the workplace that you can do better than some else. Everyone can say they are hardworking, honest, reliable, etc., but what are your skills, experience, or drive that makes you rise above the rest?

Relocation?

Finally, your relocation. Are you willing to move? Across the country, to a city? To a place in the middle of nowhere? How about to another country? Australia? The Middle East? China? South America? You need to be prepared because in our global economy these could all be viable places where you could be sent in your career. Think about your family. There are probably places where you would not want to take them. What would they do if you could only come home every six months? Military families have to think about this all the time, have you?

Career networking

Once you get your four key messages for your profile, you are ready to learn how to use LinkedIn. Remember, LinkedIn is not a social media site, it is for career networking. Once you have set up your account, go to the top of the site where it says to *search for jobs, companies and more,* put in a company you might like to work for in the future. In our case, KPMG, which is an accounting firm.

In Vince's case, he pulled it up and had 1 first degree connection and 485 second degree connections. What does that mean? It means he knows 1 person who works at KPMG and 485 people who are in that person's network. As far as third degree connections, there are 70,000 people who work at KPMG that use LinkedIn. That's a powerful network you can put right at your fingertips! So if you want a job there, 70,000 people who work there can look at your profile to see if you fit the company!

What do you want those people to think about you? A positive image on LinkedIn and mirrored on your other social media websites can send a great message to your future bosses. Now, if I follow that company, I can get updates on what is going on with that company, what their employees are doing, etc. You remember when at the end of an interview if you have any questions? This would be some great topics to talk about.

Asking for a job

Now, how else can I use LinkedIn? You may say, to get a job. NO! That is not going to work in most instances. Remember back in the networking chapter? No? Then let me explain again. Let's say a friend comes up to you and says, "Hey, I hear you work at _______, can you get me a job?" You have to say no, and being a normal human being, you feel bad about that. That's normal. Now, the next time you see that person, you're thinking, oh no, there is that person I had to say no to, I feel bad and uncomfortable around this person. Who actually likes to say no to someone? Well, unless you have the beginnings of a psychopath (in which case people probably shouldn't be around you anyway, maybe you should consider life as a hermit or something) you feel bad having to say no to someone.

Atelier_A/Shutterstock, Inc.

So, how do you use sites like LinkedIn without asking for a JOB? First, pick someone you think could be of help to you, and send him or her a message. In the message you are going to ask for "advice in my career search." This accomplishes two things simultaneously: one, you are making this person the "expert," which is good because everyone likes their ego stroked a little bit; and two, you are not asking this person for a job so he or she doesn't have to turn you down. You are simply asking for advice on your career search. Now, the expert may or may not have advice for you, but this person is under no obligation to find you a job or worse, to have to lie to you or make you feel bad. This person can freely give you advice without it being awkward. Most people will respond positively. If they don't you simply move on to the next one.

Now isn't that better than having to turn someone down or making the person or you feel bad? With this method, which you can use in a lot of different instances, you never have to worry about making those faux paus which cause many people to feel awkward. Lastly, remember this is not the time to say, "I can't contact a stranger, that's embarrassing!" To this I answer, "Get over it, this is grown up stuff. Do you really care what someone you have never met and will probably never meet cares about you? I would do handstands in public if it would get me the job and career I want!" So, put on your Big Boy or Big Girl attitude and go out here and start asking for advice!

DISCUSSION QUESTIONS

1. What is social media designed for?
2. How much does a normal person use social media (include texting, internet, etc.)?
3. How much involvement should schools get in relationship to cyberbullying? Why?
4. If a company checked your social media page, what would they find? And not find?

TERMS TO REMEMBER

Facebook	Like	YouTube
LinkedIn	Twitter	MySpace

THINGS TO REMEMBER

- Never write anything on social media that you don't want to be carved in stone forever.
- Never "badmouth" an employer or former employer.
- Red cups may be important.

REFERENCES

Smith, J. (2013, April 16). How social media can help (or hurt) your job search. Retrieved November 16, 2014, from http://www.forbes.com/sites/jacquelynsmith/2013/04/16/how-social-media-can-help-or-hurt-your-job-search/

Witsoe, Kara. (2012, March 9). Committee for Children.

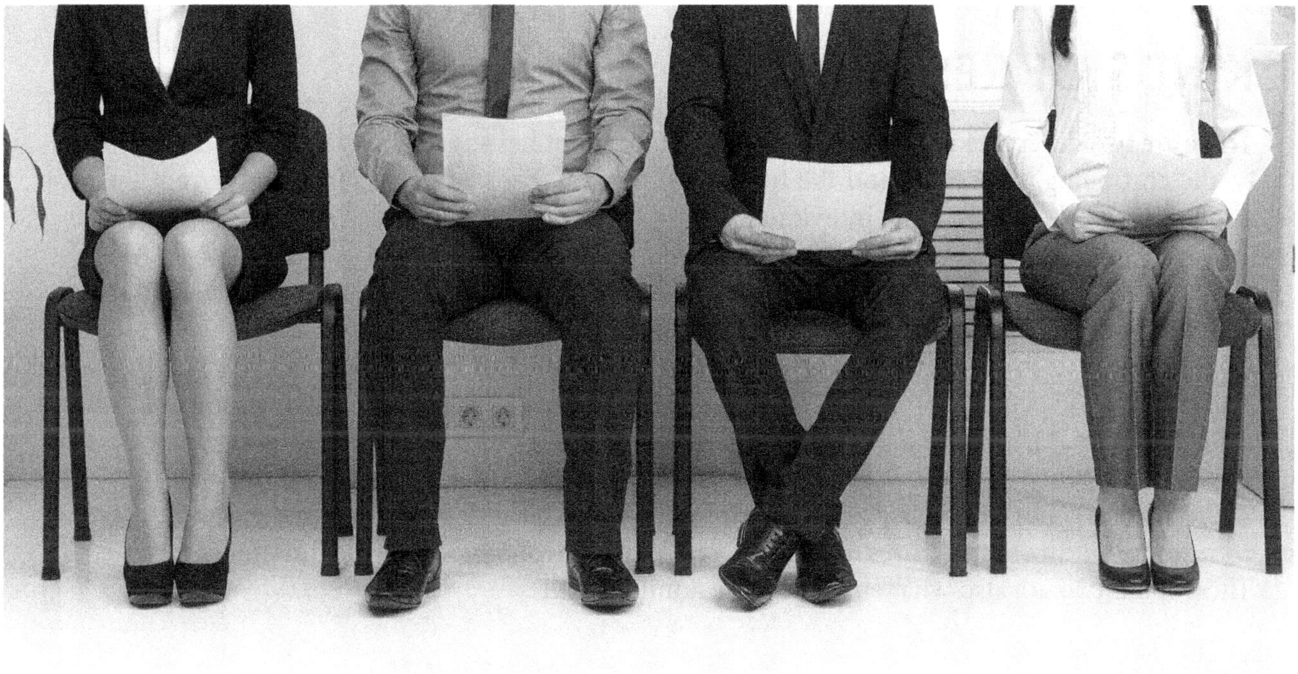

CHAPTER 5

RESUMES

A resume is an introduction of you—your skills, credentials, and accomplishments—to someone who might employ you. A resume is a fancy word for basically all of the information about you. All of your information should be on the resume so the people will get to know you, to know your skills and your background and to have an idea whether you will fit into their job needs. This is a summary of your years and must be in an easy-to-read form, yet stand out from your peers. So the resume and the next part of the process, the cover letter, is where you will tell them about this.

Simple, huh? Oh, yes, it has to fit in a one- or two-page format, be professional, concise, and true.

MAKE OR BREAK

In some ways a resume is the most important document of the job process. Hiring committees screen applicants through their resumes. If it looks like you don't have the experience they are looking for you will not be interviewed, so there goes the job. It gives the employer a sense of who you are. By looking at your past, they can infer what your future endeavors may look like. If you were in sales and increased the jig construction by 10% for XX Company, they figure that you will do the same for their company.

KINDS OF RESUMES

There are two different kinds of resumes we will talk about here as they are used most often—namely, the chronological resume and the functional resume. Each of these serves a different purpose depending on the needs of the individual.

Basically the chronological resume is a year-by-year description of the jobs you've held and a detailed description of what you've done in those jobs.

The functional resume is sometimes called a skills resume as it does just that—points out all the skills you have learned through jobs and education.

There are two other resume types that are sometimes used, the combination resume and the targeted resume, but the best features of each are part of the chronological or the functional resume, too. These main two are also what employers are familiar with.

INFORMATION

First, let's talk about the information the employer is looking for in the resume. Yes, they are looking for someone who fulfills the job description they posted, but they are also looking for someone who fits in with their present team. So the secret is to tailor your information to fit with what they are looking for plus show them you work well in a group setting with a diverse collection of people with different skills sets

NAN728/Shutterstock, Inc.

To review sample job descriptions, please follow these links:

http://hrcouncil.ca/docs/Template_JD.do

http://mrsc.org/getmedia/DE2DFF3A-E646-40A7-92A1-BC1594FB64E8/a5instr.aspx

Sample 1

The first sample is a generic one. The areas you need to look at are the summary, scope, and qualifications sections. Do you meet or exceed any of the areas? Review the skills they are looking for; do you have those skills? If so, we need to make sure they are appearing in your resume using some of the same words the job description uses.

Sample 2

The second sample is a description for a position as a Instrumentation Technician for the City of Anacortes. It explains the skills they are looking for in the position. Do these meet your requirements? Most companies and government positions have a set salary range. This is the area you will be starting at so you need to be aware of its limitations. Next, they give the general function of the job. This is the area where they give you a brief synopsis of the position. Do you meet or exceed these requirements? If not, you will probably have a hard time getting an interview.

Next are the duties and responsibilities for the position. To gain an interview you must meet these requirements. Most companies use a computer program to scan the resumes they receive for these requirements. If you don't have the qualifications for the duties and responsibilities, you probably won't even get an interview.

Using the information

So, what to do with this information? First you need to look at the job duties. In the first sample from the City of Bremerton, the first bullet under Essential Duties says, "Coordinates the development, implementation and monitoring of the City's annual budget and Capital Improvement Program." You need to mirror that in your resume.

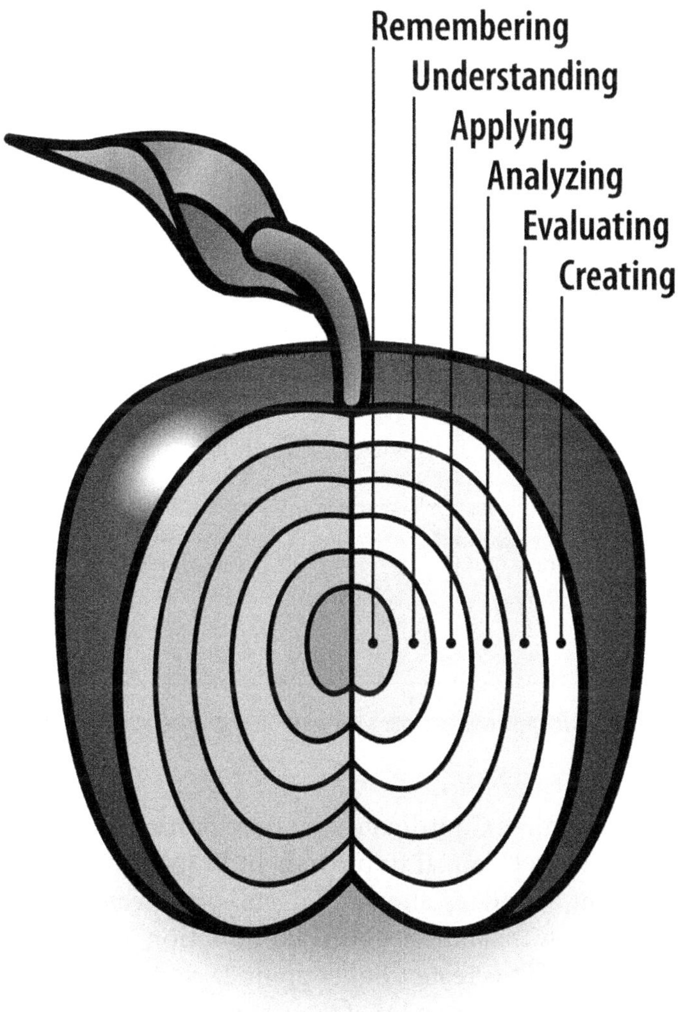

Zern Liew/Shutterstock, Inc.

Using action verbs

To mirror a job description, you need to use action verbs. The source I have found for this is Bloom's taxonomy. This is a list from Clemson University:

Definitions	Knowledge	Comprehension	Application	Analysis	Synthesis	Evaluation
Bloom's Definition	Remember previously learned information.	Demonstrate an understanding of the facts.	Apply knowledge to actual situations.	Break down objects or ideas into simpler parts and find evidence to support generalizations.	Compile component ideas into a new whole or propose alternative	Make and defend judgments based on internal evidence or external criteria.
Verbs	• Arrange • Define • Describe • Duplicate • Identify • Label • List • Match • Memorize • Name • Order • Outline • Recognize • Relate • Recall • Repeat • Reproduce • Select • State	• Classify • Convert • Defend • Describe • Discuss • Distinguish • Estimate • Explain • Express • Extend • Generalized • Give example(s) • Identify • Indicate • Infer • Locate • Paraphrase • Predict • Recognize • Rewrite • Review • Select • Summarize • Translate	• Apply • Change • Choose • Compute •Demonstrate • Discover • Dramatize • Employ • Illustrate • Interpret • Manipulate • Modify • Operate • Practice • Predict • Prepare • Produce • Relate • Schedule • Show • Sketch • Solve • Use • Write	• Analyze • Appraise • Breakdown • Calculate • Categorize • Compare • Contrast • Criticize • Diagram • Differentiate • Discriminate • Distinguish • Examine • Experiment • Identify • Illustrate • Infer • Model • Outline • Point out • Question • Relate • Select • Separate • Subdivide • Test	• Arrange • Assemble • Categorize • Collect • Combine • Comply • Compose • Construct • Create • Design • Develop • Devise • Explain • Formulate • Generate • Plan • Prepare • Rearrange • Reconstruct • Relate • Reorganize • Revise • Rewrite • Set up • Summarize • Synthesize • Tell • Write	• Appraise • Argue • Assess • Attach • Choose • Compare • Conclude • Contrast • Defend • Describe • Discriminate • Estimate • Evaluate • Explain • Judge • Justify • Interpret • Relate • Predict • Rate • Select • Summarize • Support • Value

http://www.clemson.edu/assessment/assessmentpractices/referencematerials/documents/Blooms%20Taxonomy%20Action%20Verbs.pdf

From the first sample, the new hire "Coordinates the development, implementation and monitoring of the City's annual budget and Capital Improvement Program." What words could be used to describe this skill? How about, "Produce annual budgets" or "Create budgets for capital improvement programs"? Do you see how that is done? You take an action verb from Bloom's taxonomy and you combine it with a needed skill to create a bullet point. If you do this for the skills that match up in the job description, you will soon have a lot of your resume filled out.

CHRONOLOGICAL RESUME

The chronological resume is the one most often used and is the resume that is sometimes required. The chronological resume lists your previous jobs in year by year order, beginning with the most recent.

On the top of the resume, you put your name, address, phone number, and email address. If you don't have an email address you need to make one. There are numerous sites where can get you one, and yes they are free (for instance, Yahoo!, Gmail which is Google mail, Hotmail). There are a lot of them. However, let me give you a note of caution: please make your email name sound professional, especially since you can have several email accounts. Hotgirl or guy69.com is obviously not a professional email and definitely won't get you the job.

Objectives

Next in the chronological resume is what's called the objective, or a statement of the kind of position you're looking for now. Conventional wisdom says you don't really need an objective anymore. In the past, the objective was important when you were sending out the same resume for all positions because they were made on a typewriter and it was hard to customize each one. Now, when you're pretty much going to tailor each resume for the company, you really don't need the objective. For example, let's say when looking for a position of electronics technician, you are going to make your resume specifically for that job description, so do you really need an objective? It should be obvious what position you are going for through the resume and cover letter.

However, and this is a big however, some employers look for an objective. My recommendation is that you write one (even if you know it's not needed) rather than get your resume tossed out by HR when they couldn't find one.

Employment information

Next in the chronological resume is your employment information. Start from your job you are now working (if you are working), then your previous one before that, and so on. How far do you go back? Rule of thumb is five years unless a particular job you held will be a factor in the new job. Some companies may ask for ten years of previous employment information.

Under the employer's name should be your job title, the dates when you worked there (month and year is fine, for example 3/12 to 3/14 for March 2012 to March 2014), and a little bit of information about what you did at that position. Sometimes this past job will seem to have nothing to do with the job you are applying for, however you can fix this. For example, let's say you were working at Subway Sandwich shop; nothing to do with say, an electronics position, right? Wrong. You can always find things to put down from a previous job. Think about the new job you are applying for—What are they looking for? (If you don't know, do some research at places like O-Net, http://www.onetonline.org/.) So, if the job description is for someone who can work with other people on a team, then say things like: achieved a particular amount of sales, trained in customer service, gave excellent service to customers, and made excellent detailed notes on phone calls. All of these are skills I daresay any organization would want in their employees. So, your previous jobs do have some value even if you don't have practical experience in the field you are entering.

Sample

Name
[Street Address, City, ST ZIP Code] • [Phone number] • [E-mail]

Objective [Describe your career goal or ideal job.]

Experience

[Job Title]
[Company Name], [City, ST]
[Start date] – [End date]

[Job responsibility/achievement]

[Job responsibility/achievement]

[Job responsibility/achievement]

[Job Title]
[Company Name], [City, ST]
[Start date] – [End date]

[Job responsibility/achievement]

[Job responsibility/achievement]

[Job responsibility/achievement]

[Job Title]
[Company Name], [City, ST]
[Start date] – [End date]

[Job responsibility/achievement]

[Job responsibility/achievement]

[Job responsibility/achievement]

[Job Title]
[Company Name], [City, ST]
[Start date] – [End date]

[Job responsibility/achievement]

[Job responsibility/achievement]

[Job responsibility/achievement]

Education

[Degree obtained]
[School Name], [City, ST]
[Date graduated]

[Special award/accomplishment or degree minor]

Interests [Briefly list interests that might pertain to the job you want.]

References References are available on request.

Employment gaps

What about employment gaps? If you were out of work, or if you were in school, explain those gaps right in the resume because the disparity of time will be noticed. (If you were slumped in a chair watching TV for two years you might seriously consider using a functional resume.) In the chronological resume what should ultimately emerge is a detailed accounting of your past few years in the workplace.

Education

Your education will be in chronological order as well. The most recent school and what degree you will have when you graduate goes first. Include any college you might have had including when you will graduate if you have not graduated yet. Also list any certificates you have earned.

Next will be high school or GED. Don't worry, everybody pretty much all graduated with a general studies degree from high school, so unless you went to one of those special technical high schools you probably just can list a high school diploma. Remember to put in the month and year you graduated.

Interests

The interests section can be used to convey other interests. If you have room, this is where you will list if you speak other languages or if you are particularly proud of an accomplishment like Eagle Scout or that you were an ambassador at your school or you were student body president in high school.

General tips

You may go more than one page if it is warranted. But, you have to have enough information to fill the space. You may not do it with just fancy fonts or big headings. You need to remember this resume is not for you. **The resume is for the reader**. So, if you want to send it in a font color or use a fancy font, *forget it.* Chances are the resume will eventually be read by someone with a very busy schedule, a definite sense of professionalism, and no sense of humor.

FUNCTIONAL RESUME

The functional resume is also sometimes called the skills resume. The skills resume is just that—instead of highlighting your past work experience, you want to highlight the skills you have developed. This kind of resume is mostly used for jobs that require specific skills. For example, if you are a computer person with a background in software development of games and you are applying for a job with a games company, a functional resume will highlight those skills and experiences you have. The company is not interested so much in your job at the coffee shop that put you through school, but they need to know about your skills in developing computer games. So, as before you want to look in the job description for the skills and duties they are looking for in an applicant and tailor your resume to meet those needs.

Specifics

The top part of the functional resume is the same as the chronological resume: you put your name, address, phone number, and a professional email address there. You will then start listing your skills—things you have done in labs or things that you have done while in school or in previous jobs. Always be aware that you are applying for a specific job with a specific company that has a description of the job for hire. You want to talk in detail about how your particular abilities and talents give you the expertise to fit their needs.

[Your Name]
[Street Address, City, ST ZIP Code] [phone] [email]

Objective	[Briefly describe your career goal or ideal job]		
Professional Achievements	**[Field or Area of Accomplishment]** • [Achievement] • [Achievement] • [Achievement] **[Field or Area of Accomplishment]** • [Achievement] • [Achievement] • [Achievement] **[Field or Area of Accomplishment]** • [Achievement] • [Achievement] • [Achievement] **[Field or Area of Accomplishment]** • [Achievement] • [Achievement] • [Achievement]		
Skills	• [Professional or technical skill] • [Professional or technical skill] • [Professional or technical skill] • [Professional or technical skill]	• [Professional or technical skill] • [Professional or technical skill] • [Professional or technical skill] • [Professional or technical skill]	
Work History	[Job Title]	[Company Name], [City, ST]	[Dates]
	[Job Title]	[Company Name], [City, ST]	[Dates]
	[Job Title]	[Company Name], [City, ST]	[Dates]
	[Job Title]	[Company Name], [City, ST]	[Dates]
Education	[Degree]	[School Name], [City, ST]	[Date of graduation]
References	References are available on request.		

Using action verbs

Just like in the chronological resume, you want to use Bloom's taxonomy to focus on the skills that are in the job description and address those skills on your resume using action verbs. So if you are applying for an electronics technician, and the job wants you to be able to calibrate a certain kind of equipment, you may put, "I can calibrate this type of equipment" or "I can perform this test."

Here is a link to some sample functional resumes: http://www.vault.com/resumes/sample/functional-resumes/functional-resume 01

Your Name

Street Number and name, City, State, Zip Code
E-Mail Address Telephone: (111) 111-1111

Objective

Example: Actively seeking to provide exemplary service in an institution which will allow utilization of leadership skills.

Education

Degree – Major
College/University – Your City, State — Sept 2003 – Aug 2007

Summary of Skills & Capabilities

- Type your skills and capabilities in these bullet points
- Bellow are some examples
- Self-manager with a strong sense of commitment to quality work.
- Multifaceted, team player and able to adapt to new environments.
- Excellent planning, prioritizing and organizing skills.
- Competent in typing, compiling, editing and proofreading reports, letters, memos and forms. Extremely proficient in MS Word, Excel and PowerPoint.
- Effectively perform tasks and interact with others using excellent written and oral communication skills.

Employment History

State your Position
Company Name, City located, STATE — Feb 2008 – July 2008

- Here you type in your roles and responsibilities
- Limit it to three points, keep it brief and concise
- Use powerful words such as managed, pioneered, tracked, productivity, organization, etc.

Company Name, City located, STATE — Feb 2008 – July 2008

- Here you type in your roles and responsibilities
- Limit it to three points, keep it brief and concise
- Use powerful words such as managed, pioneered, tracked, productivity, organization, etc.

Company Name, City located, STATE — Feb 2008 – July 2008

- Here you type in your roles and responsibilities
- Limit it to three points, keep it brief and concise
- Use powerful words such as managed, pioneered, tracked, productivity, organization, etc.

References

Available upon request.

Remember, you are not reinventing the wheel; it is OK to go on the internet, search for "sample resumes" and see what wording other people have used. This should give you a wealth of ideas.

DISCUSSION QUESTIONS

1. What are the pros and cons of using the chronological resume?
2. Under what circumstances would a functional resume be best to use?
3. Discuss in detail the use of Bloom's taxonomy.
4. Explain how to handle time gaps in your resume.

TERMS TO REMEMBER

Chronological	Gaps	Functional
Service	Internet	Action verbs

THINGS TO REMEMBER

- Avoid fancy fonts or colors.
- Keep customers happy so they remain customers.
- Keep e-mail names professional.

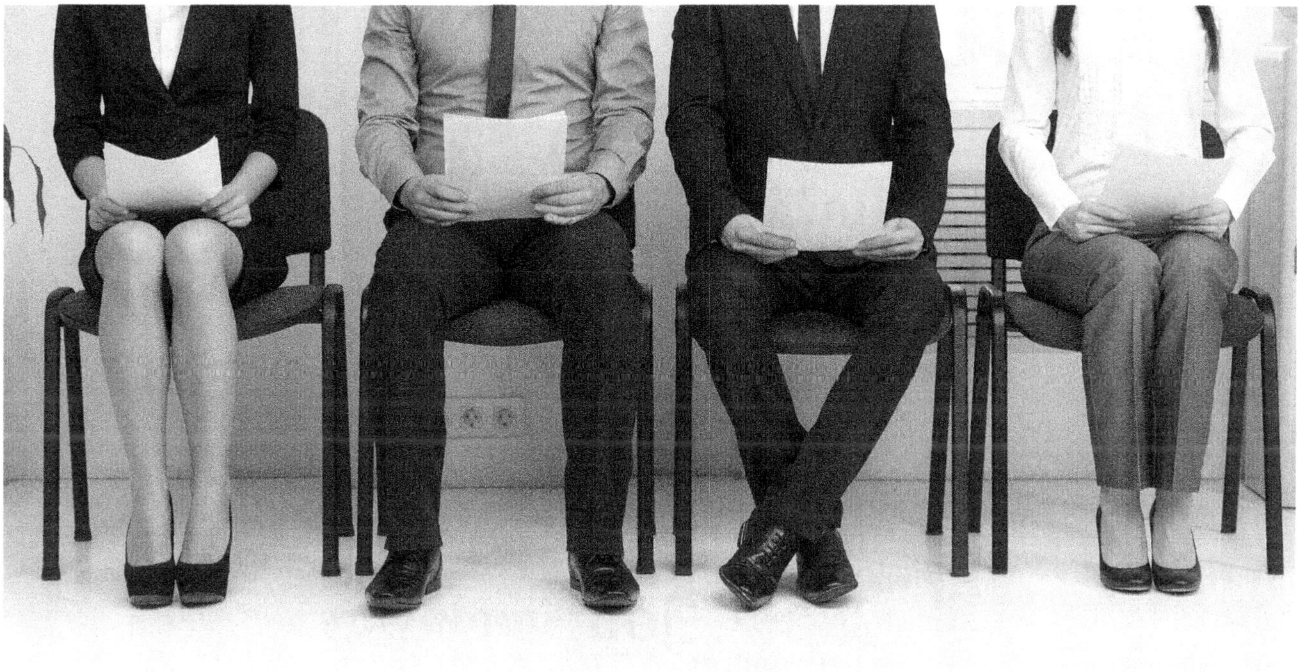

CHAPTER 6

COVER LETTERS AND REFERENCES

COVER LETTERS

A cover letter is a brief introduction to a potential employer. It explains who you are, what job you are applying for, your qualifications for that job, and a request for an interview. Your cover letter must be interesting enough for whoever is reading it to want to pass it up the ladder. The bottom line is to get your resume read and ultimately to get an interview. The cover letter is the first impression that a prospective employer has of you and if you are fit for a new hire. It must garner attention, give pertinent information, and persuade the reader to look more closely at your attached resume.

Different strokes

Each cover letter will be different as each company's hiring needs are different. This is very important. Do not do a quick cut and paste job to change a little information. Give some time and energy into looking at what each company wants and shape your cover letter (and later your resume) to answer their specific needs. No company wants a hurried, thrown-together response; their thinking will be that you personally are of the same ilk. In other words, if your resume or cover letter is sloppy, they think you are, too.

Oh, it must be all on one page and the briefer the better. Easy, huh!

Rafal Olechowski/Shutterstock, Inc.

Must I?

Many people ask, "Do I have to have a cover letter?" The answer is yes. Some employers won't look at a resume without a cover letter. Some glance briefly at it to check qualifications before moving on to the resume. Still others ignore it completely. My rule is that it is better to have one and not need it than to need it and not have it. Best policy is to do everything by the book. Sometimes that is a pain in the butt but it might make the difference in whether you get an interview or not. No interview equals no job.

Reasons

YuryZap/Shutterstock, Inc.

A little secret knowledge on why you not only need to have a cover letter but to do the research on it at the same time. Many companies now use a program, an algorithm, to scan cover letters and resumes. It scans for keywords that are listed on the job posting or description. By scanning this information, they can see if the applicant has the skills they need for the position. Now, if you didn't do the research and put in the keywords, your cover letter or resume might not even be looked at by a human being! Sucks, huh? You might be the perfect person for the position and the company, and if you don't use the right words, you never get your shot at an interview.

Research

Your cover letter and resume is written to a particular company for a specific job. As in your resume, the more knowledgeable you are about the company of your potential employer the better versed in honing your cover letter. Check the company's website for information on the organization's future goals. Spend some time on the internet reviewing similar companies until you have an understanding of the role your potential company plays overall.

What makes this company tick?

Read up on the power structure of the company, taking note of how each department plays into the other. If possible, find out who will be reading your cover letter and address it directly to this person; sometimes a phone call to the secretary provides that information. This shows that you have invested time and energy and want to become a part of the team.

Callahan/Shutterstock, Inc.

Speaking of the power structure

Wisdom

A word to the wise about your relationship with secretaries and receptionists in general. Always, always be super polite and grateful for any help the secretary/receptionist gives you. They will most often help everyone, but for the people they like personally they can do so much more. They work directly with the decision makers. A negative comment made to a potential employer reiterates any negative thinking; the positive comment does the same thing. My father always called the front desks personnel of any agency the "gatekeepers," which pretty much says it all.

Practicalities

Whether your cover letter and resume are written or e-mailed, the same rules apply; they must be concise, brief, and tailored to a specific company where you are applying. If you are e-mailing it, I recommend that you also send one by regular mail. E-mail boxes of busy people become cluttered and it never hurts to draw positive attention to yourself twice.

The cover letter is the first thing a hiring agent sees; if there are any

Typos
Incorrect use of words
Hard to read font
Cluttered, cramped layout
Colored ink
Small points
Repeat of resume

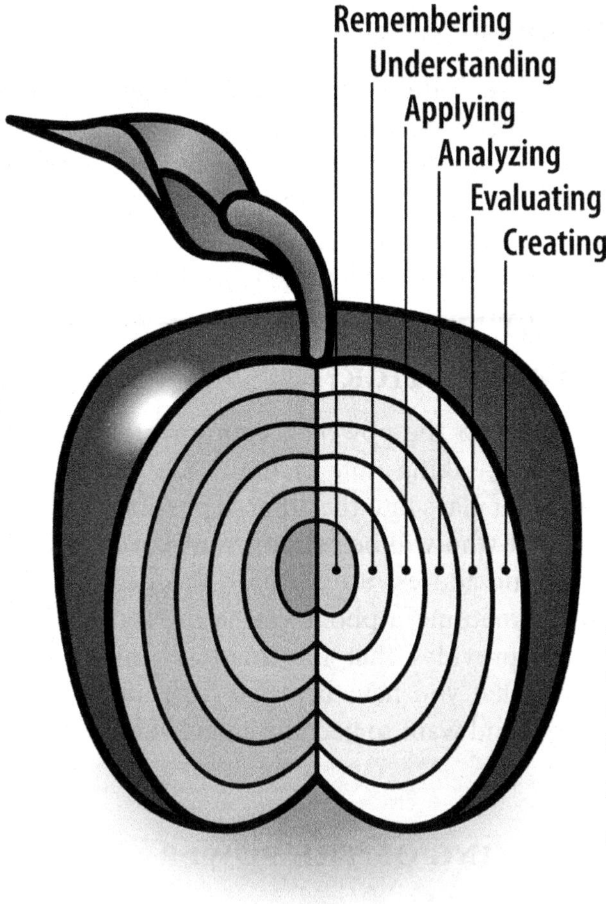

Zern Liew/Shutterstock, Inc.

Then you can probably bet that it's dropped in the wastebasket. Employers and their agents have little time and lots of applications. Leave plenty of white space and make it easy enough to read for your elderly grandmother. ***Appearance is essential.***

Bloom's taxonomy

As mentioned, Bloom's taxonomy is a list of words that are extremely useful in a cover letter and resume. One of the best lists is from the Iowa State University Center for Excellence in Learning and Teaching. It can be found at: http://www.celt.iastate.edu/teaching-resources/effective-practice/revised-blooms-taxonomy/blooms-model-text/

Here are a few samples:

Know		Comprehend	
Count	Read	Classify	Interpret
Define	Recall	Cite	Locate
Describe	Recite	Conclude	Make sense of
Enumerate	Record	Describe	Paraphrase
Find	Reproduce	Discuss	Predict
Identify	Select	Estimate	Report
Label	Sequence	Explain	Restate
List	State	Generalize	Review
Match	View	Give examples	Summarize
Name	Write	Illustrate	Trace
Apply		**Analyze**	
Assess	Instruct	Break down	Examine
Change	Predict	Characterize	Illustrate
Chart	Prepare	Classify	Infer
Choose	Produce	Compare	Limit
Compute	Relate	Contrast	Outline
Construct	Report	Correlate	Point out
Demonstrate	Select	Diagram	Prioritize
Determine	Show	Differentiate	Relate
Develop	Solve	Discriminate	Separate
Establish	Use	Distinguish	Subdivide
Synthesize		**Evaluate**	
Adapt	Invent	Appraise	Interpret
Categorize	Modify	Argue	Judge
Compose	Organize	Assess	Justify
Construct	Perform	Choose	Predict
Create	Produce	Compare & Contrast	Prioritize
Design	Propose	Conclude	Prove
Formulate	Reinforce	Critique	Rank
Generate	Reorganize	Decide	Rate
Incorporate	Rewrite	Defend	Reframe
Integrate	Structure	Evaluate	Support

Also check out onetonline.org—a must use site! This site has all kinds of occupations and examples of words to use. Review the sample job description from the website here:

49-9043.00 - Maintenance Workers, Machinery

Lubricate machinery, change parts, or perform other routine machinery maintenance.

Following are examples of the tasks required for a machinery maintenance worker. For more detailed information including knowledge, skills, abilities, work activities, work context, job zone, interests, work values, work needs, and related occupations, visit the O*Net web site at http://online.onetcenter.org.

Tasks

- Sets up and operates machine and adjusts controls that regulate operational functions to ensure conformance to specifications.
- Lubricates, oils, or applies adhesive, or other material to machines, machine parts, or other equipment, according to specified procedures.
- Starts machine and observes mechanical operation to determine efficiency and to detect defects, malfunctions, or other machine damage.
- Installs, replaces, or changes machine parts and attachments, according to production specifications.
- Replaces or repairs metal, wood, leather, glass, or other lining in machine or equipment compartments or containers.
- Dismantles machine, removes machine parts, and reassembles machine, using hand tools, chain falls, jack, crane, or hoist.
- Cleans machine and machine parts, using cleaning solvent, cloth, air gun, hose, vacuum, or other equipment.
- Removes hardened material from machine or machine parts, using abrasives, power and hand tools, jackhammer, sledgehammer, or other equipment.
- Collects and discards worn machine parts and other garbage to maintain machinery and work areas.
- Transports machine parts, tools, equipment and other material between work areas and storage, using crane, hoist, or dolly.
- Inventories and requisitions machine parts, equipment, and other supplies to replenish and maintain stock.
- Records and maintains production, repair, and machine maintenance information.
- Marks, separates, ties, aligns, threads, attaches, or inserts material or product preparatory to machine operation or to identify machine process.
- Measures, mixes, prepares and tests chemical solutions used to clean or repair machinery and equipment, according to product specifications.
- Communicates with or assists other workers to repair or move machines, machine parts or equipment.
- Replaces, empties, or replenishes empty machine and equipment containers, such as gas tanks or boxes.

- Reads work orders and specifications to determine machines and equipment requiring repair or maintenance.
- Cuts, shapes, smoothes, attaches or assembles pieces of metal, wood, rubber, or other material repair and maintenance machines and equipment.
- Inspects or tests damaged machine parts and marks defective area or advises supervisor of need for repair.

See the highlighted section? If you can do those things, they need to appear in your cover letter. If they don't, they need to be in your resume. These are the keywords the algorithm keyword program is looking for.

WHAT GOES WHERE?

At the top of the page list your name, address, phone number, and e-mail address. Reminder: use a phone number where you can be reached all the time. It's frustrating for employers when they decide to ask you a further question and cannot reach you. They may just move to the next person on the list.

Your greeting should be professional.

Dear Mr. Joe Doe:

You will get this personal information from a company website, a secretary, or goggle search. This target approach must not be familiar like "Hello Joe" or even "Hi Mr. Doe." In all your writings, whether resume, applications, or cover letters, keep it on a professional level. This indicates to the potential employer that you are mature, and will be a good representative for the company. If you absolutely no way can find a real person to address your cover letter to, then don't give any greeting. A "To Whom It May Concern" or "Dear Sir or Madam" is too generic and unrefined. Use "Dear Human Resources" or "Dear Personnel Manager" if you must use a salutation.

Provide a sentence or two about what position you are applying for and where you found the information about the job. Be specific, the employer may other positions advertized. If a friend told you about the job, give your friend's name of the friend and relate if he is employed with that particular company.

Give your qualifications and how you are well suited for the position. Be positive and enthusiastic; this is the time for you to show off your selling points. Put your qualifications in bullets with short concise sentences, addressing the needs of the employer. Add that your resume is enclosed.

Always close by thanking employers for their time and invite them to contact you. You can also give a time in which you will contact them. I recommend that you add something like, "If you need any further information, please contact me at telephone number 000-000."

End with either "Regards" or "Sincerely"

Sign with ink pen.

SAMPLE COVER LETTERS

Here are links to two examples of what a cover letter should look like:

http://jobsearch.about.com/od/academic/fl/academic-cover-letter-example.htm

http://www.vanderbilt.edu/career/tools/cover-letters.php (from Vanderbilt University; cover letters are at the bottom of the page)

Sample from Microsoft Word

For easy access to samples, use Microsoft Word. Just don't leave it as is and put your information in, because thousands of people have used these and it looks bad if yours looks like everyone else's. To get them, go to Microsoft Word, go to File, New, and type in Cover Letters; then do the search, and enjoy. There are a lot of them!

Resources

There are a multitude of free resources and many books written on just cover letters. They are mostly similar but some are very detailed. For example, Martin Yates from the *New York Times* "Knock 'em Dead" series covers every contingency known to man. Most of you need a basic cover letter and some creativity. Other cover letter articles and templates can be found on the internet. Do a search for "sample cover letters" on Google or your favorite search engine. Be careful, there are some sites that will want to charge you for them, but don't do it! There are all kinds of them up on the internet for free. If in doubt, stick to ones that have .edu on the end, they are reserved for educational use so there won't be a charge.

REFERENCES

General knowledge

First there are a few things you should know about recommendations in general and letters of recommendation specifically. In the last decade there has been a rash of lawsuits about former employers' negative comments and their ensuing impact. Because of this, many companies, especially in the public sector, only give out whether the person was ever employed there or not. Occasionally, there will be a further question of "would you rehire so-and-so or not?" and most companies have a policy not to go there but some will answer that question.

Real-time references

*Your job references **will** be called*. Those references are important and what they say about you counts. In general your references should include your work as part of a team, your relationship with your direct supervisor, and any unique projects you had a hand in. In other words, a new hire needs what is called soft skills; other proficiencies can be taught if the basic ability is there.

Wait until asked

Wait until prospective employers ask for references. Usually this means that you are in the top tier for employment at their company. They will usually ask for three references; I try to have four at my fingertips. There will be an error on one or another will be on the bland side so having a backup relieves my stress level. Another way I reduce tension is to ask the people who are writing my letters of recommendation to call me after a potential employer calls them. That lets me know that I'm still on the playing field.

Honesty

I can't emphasize enough the need for honesty. Yes, you can slant your skills and abilities toward answering certain questions but you cannot tell an untruth. Not only will you not get the job but you will be talked about in the industry. Little lies are the same as big lies and they will all hurt you. It's not worth it.

Now who do I ask?

I am always asked, "Who should I ask for references—my professor, my friend, my priest?" How about none of the above. Employers wouldn't believe your friend (I certainly wouldn't). I would believe your priest but he sees only a fraction of who you are. Your professor can only relate (with your permission) your grade and academic skills. None of these individuals, however, can tell your potential employers what they want to know regarding your skills and work ethic, how you react at work to diversity, and what role you would play on a team (leader, loner, or negotiator).

Best recommendation givers

The best people for you to ask to write you a letter of reference are present or former employers. They can answer all the questions a prospective employer asks. First, you ask if they would be willing to write you a letter of recommendation. If they are reluctant, don't push it—a negative or neutral letter is poison.

If they consent, give them your resume to use. I also suggest that you include two other items: a copy of the job description of the position you are applying for, and what I call an "info letter." I learned to use this info letter because sometimes my former boss who was fabulous as a leader couldn't write worth squat (and knew it). He asked me if I would create some points that he could use for that particular application. That worked great as it was slanted toward a specific job. By providing them a letter of information you are guiding them toward answering the specifics of the company's advertised requirements. I use key words taken from the job description itself to connect the employer's job description with the letter of recommendation.

Sample for reference page

[Your Name]
[Street Address]
[City, ST ZIP Code]
[Phone]
[Email]

References:
[Reference Name]
[Title]
[Company Name]
[Street Address]
[City, ST ZIP Code]
[Phone]
[Email]

Relationship: [Relationship with reference] at [Company Name] from [dates of employment]

[Reference Name]
[Title]
[Company Name]
[Street Address]
[City, ST ZIP Code]
[Phone]
[Email]

Relationship: [Relationship with reference] at [Company Name] from [dates of employment]

[Reference Name]
[Title]
[Company Name]
[Street Address]
[City, ST ZIP Code]
[Phone]
[Email]

Relationship: [Relationship with reference] at [Company Name] from [dates of employment]

DISCUSSION QUESTIONS

1. What do you expect your cover letter to do for you?
2. What is the need for Bloom's taxonomy?
3. Who should I ask to write my references?
4. Why can't I cut and paste a cover letter?

TERMS TO REMEMBER

Gatekeepers	Info letter	Job references
Bloom's taxonomy	Algorithm	Slant info

THINGS TO REMEMBER

- Your cover letter is written to a particular company for a particular job.
- Your appearances is essential.
- References will be checked.
- Be honest, because lies aren't worth it.

REFERENCE

Microsoft Office Templates

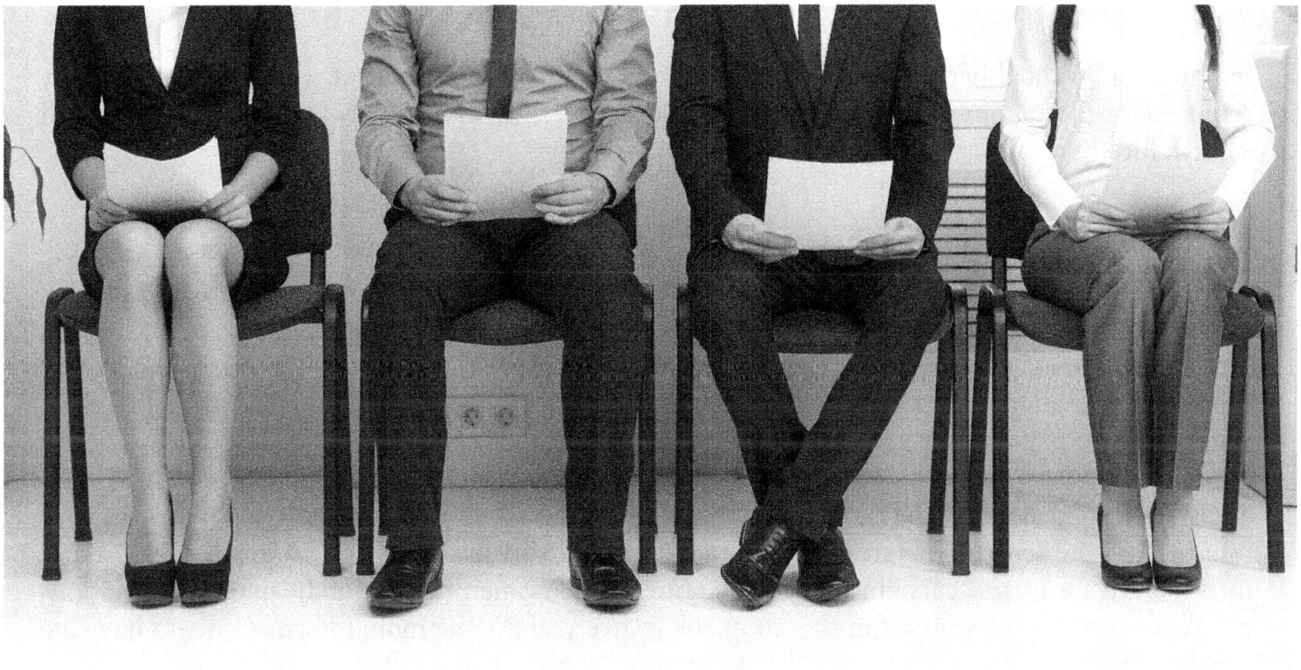

CHAPTER 7

STANDARD INTERVIEW

HOW IT WORKS

You've gotten this far; obviously they liked your resume or some other trait about you; now you must prepare for the face-to-face interview. There are two main types of interviews you'll encounter in today's job market—the standard interview and the behavioral interview. This chapter will focus on the standard interview and the next chapter will focus on the behavioral interview. You need to be prepared to function with either type, or a combination of both. Older companies and school districts still focus on the standard interview process with a few behavioral questions thrown in.

Depending on the job, you will usually be competing against three to five other candidates; the paper process will have narrowed the field. The first interview will narrow that to two or three people and those will be called back for a second and final interview.

In a small company, or a two-person show, the employer may interview you directly; usually a more casual environment and the decision to hire or not may be immediate. Sydney G. was looking for part-time employment and met a friend for lunch in an ice cream parlor. She asked the waitress if the parlor would be hiring for part-time and summer employment. It turned out the waitress was the boss and wanted her to return the next day when the little restaurant wasn't so busy. Sydney returned for the appointment and was hired. It sometimes works like that—a good impression and a quick hire.

Research

In most jobs, however, you're going to need to do some research before you get there. The company website will give you the overall facts and data of what this company does, its goals, and its history. You should have a thorough knowledge of the company before the interview. There's no excuse nowadays with all the information on the internet for being unaware of a company's division, what products the company may use, and the sources where they're obtained.

You should know not only the name of the CEO or the head of the company, but a rough map in your mind of how the departments are laid out and interrelated. You need to know exactly what the company is looking for in new personnel and their future goals. (Sometimes one of the interview questions is: "Where do you see yourself in this company in five years?" The more information you have the more comprehensive you can answer the question. Keep notes in a small notebook if you don't have a good memory; it is not taboo to refer to it during the interview if you have to. As an employer, I would rather the person look in the notebook than stare at me blankly and say, "I don't know."

Late is the kiss of death

One of the first rules of the interview process is *never ever ever* be late for an interview. There is absolutely no excuse that is acceptable. It shows a lack of respect for both the interviewer and the job. It shows that you're not a person to be trusted; and it shows a lack of integrity and trust.

I recommend that as soon as you know what day your interview will be, you start making plans—at least a week before. If you know where the interview will take place and it is local, you drive by the week before to check out the traffic and available parking. If the interview is in another city where you must take an airplane, try to get there early the day before the interview. I recommend that you do a reconnaissance of the place; you know, scope it out so that you can see where you're going, what the traffic is like. If you are coming from a smaller city to a larger city you must take into account things like rush-hour traffic and freeway stoppages. (Los Angeles comes immediately to mind.) You always want to leave yourself plenty of time to get to the interview even if you have to wait for a few minutes in your car. It's better to get there and wait for 30 minutes than it is for you to be even a moment late. Late in a very bad economy pretty much ensures that even if the employer interviews you, there is a large question mark on your reliability.

Appropriate dress

You need to dress appropriately for each interview. A good basic rule of thumb is to dress one level up from what you would expect to wear on your first day of work. If you are interviewing for a professional job (like a financial planner or something along those lines), you would dress differently than if you were interviewing for a tech job in Silicon Valley. If you are in doubt what employees in the company wear, check out its website to see what others are wearing. Remember they are interviewing you to see if you are a good fit for their company so you need for your dress to reflect that.

Personal style that is the latest "in" thing goes out the window. For men and women, this is not the time to make a fashion statement or prove that you can wear whatever you want. Error on the side of conservativism. I think someone famous said, "If in doubt, don't."

Clothes prep

A week or two before the interview is scheduled, I recommend getting out what I call my interview clothes to check them out. Try them on, make sure they still fit, and that nothing is stained. It is essential that your grooming is first rate. If you have facial hair, it must be neatly trimmed; if you need a haircut, get one several days before the interview.

We all have what we call our regular Sunday best. Sometimes this is a good outfit for interviews. It is carved in stone that you wear nothing that distracts from your presentation.

For the men:

- Wear khakis or slacks and a long-sleeve dress shirt with or without a sport coat for semiprofessional or professional job requirements. (I recommend wearing a white t-shirt under the dress shirt if it's thin. No one wants to see your hairy chest.) Ties are optional unless you are interviewing for a professional job that requires you to wear one most days of employment.
- If you are applying for a job that entails physical labor, pressed khakis are still okay as are good jeans with a nice polo shirt or dress shirt.
- Shoes must be clean and polished if possible. It's amazing how many people judge others on their shoes.
- No jewelry or piercings at an interview. It may turn off an employer. After you are hired, you can revisit that rule.
- No ragged or tight jeans. No shorts (even nice ones).
- Tennis shoes are not appropriate unless you are applying for a job at a gym or they are leather and can pass as shoes.
- Do not smoke before an interview; it remains on your clothes even if you can't smell it.
- Do not chew gum.

For the women:

- Same rules apply as for the men. Do not wear anything that distracts from your presentation. It's all about getting hired.
- Wear clean, well-fitting clothes. Dresses or pant suits are appropriate for most job interviews as are slacks and a nice top. It is not the time for a fashion statement; you want to fit in, not stand out.
- Keep makeup light, especially if you're interviewing for a large company where the hiring is done by human resource personnel. They will have a large base of potential employees to choose from.
- Earrings are okay but take out the eyebrow, tongue, nose jewelry. It may make the wrong statement to an employer.

- Avoid showing cleavage. You want to keep the focus on your job skills.
- No bra straps should show. Again, some employees may be turned off.
- No 4-inch heels; you wouldn't wear them to work anyway, so this is not the time to show off your shoe collection.
- No tight jeans (even colored ones) or shorts (not even nice ones).
- Tennis shoes are not appropriate unless you are applying at a gym; neither are flip-flops (not even jeweled ones).
- Do not smoke before an interview because the smell clings to clothes.
- Do not chew gum.

EARLY BIRDS

One of the reasons for arriving at the place where you will be interviewed 15 minutes early is if the interviewers are running early, they may be able to take you right away and that's always a good thing. It lets them know that you are punctual, eager, and adaptable. It also lets them know that you're going to be the person who is always on time for work.

Gatekeepers

There is usually a secretary or receptionist who will greet you and tell you where to wait. This is a *very* important person, because he or she has the ear of the boss and can be a deciding factor in your employment. One negative comment between the receptionist and the boss can kill your chances if there is someone else you are competing closely with. If the receptionist is busy, do not engage in conversation or ask questions. Smile pleasantly and stay seated. If the receptionist wants to chat, be congenial and nice.

Do not tease, flirt, try to charm, or be unfriendly. My father always says that receptionists and nurses run the world. Or at least they make a major impact on it.

Nonverbal communication

When you walk into the interview, keep your head up. With confidence greet each interviewer after being introduced with whatever name each was introduced to you. If you know "Mark" and he's introduced as "Mr. Webster," then you greet him as "Mr. Webster." Lean forward and give each person a good handshake. If the interviewer is female, then follow her lead: either step forward and shake hands if she does or simply nod and smile if she does this instead. Regardless of gender, don't do what I call the little fish handshake. Shake hands firmly; neither with a limp wrist nor so strongly that it's a show of force. You're here to make a good impression with all things you do. Just give a firm handshake and that's it. You don't need to prove anything.

Sit down with your feet flat on the floor if you can. Put your hands flat on the table. If you need to hold onto your other hand because you're shaking a little bit that's very acceptable. Most people who interview others are experienced and understand that you're going to be nervous. It's okay to be nervous but waving your hands all over the place is distracting. Better to clasp your hands together to cease their movements.

You want to appear confident in your abilities and you need to portray that nonverbally in the interview. And you *never* interrupt. With some of us eager-beaver hyperactive people, that's hard. Answer the questions that are asked fully, but do not waste the interviewers' time with extemporaneous additions.

Standard interview committees

There are certain questions that most employers or their representatives ask in a standard interview. If there are several people interviewing you, they will most likely have a set of questions in front of them. They will take turns asking questions. For example, Mrs. Smith might ask questions 3, 4, and 9, which are questions about subjects in the field where she is very knowledgeable. If there are several people at the interview table they will most likely be working with a matrix that scores answers from their perspective. After all the interviews are complete they will compare scores to choose their potential employee.

Responses

Do not volunteer answers to questions that have not been asked. Try not to ramble. The most likely first question will be for you to tell them about yourself. Basically what they want to know is *what there is in your background and experience that will help them further their bottom line*—no matter what that is. They have your resume so you don't need to repeat that.

You need to tell them how your past experiences have prepared you for a good fit of whatever they are looking for. If there's something unique about you, this is the time to disclose it, even if it was part of your resume. For example, a blond-haired friend speaks fluent Hopi; his Native American grandmother taught him. A girl I know is a dental assistant but can use all kinds of power tools and her hobby is building cabinets. Anything that's distinctive makes them remember you; a unique identifier.

If there is a nice accomplishment that you are particularly proud of that will make you stand out in their mind, this is the time to advise them of it, especially volunteer work. If you spent time developing an afterschool program or volunteering to teach swim lessons at the Y, tell them. No bragging, just state the facts. And the facts will be checked to assure if it is a truth. BOTTOM LINE, SAY WHAT YOU HAVE TO SAY AND THEN,"SHUT UP." I was on an interview panel where we asked a lady to tell us about herself, and she talked for 20 minutes!

BOTTOM LINE

All questions asked during a standard interview are basically the same; if we hire you, how are you going to help the company/store/business? That's what they really want to know. Do you have abilities or potential abilities to make this company better? What can you do better than someone else? It's great if you can talk about numbers—people remember numbers, so quantify if you can. "At my last job I improved efficiency and productivity by 20%." Or, "I was in the top five in my class of computer repair." Or, "I placed first [or second] in a skills competition for ARC welding." People are trained to remember numbers so you want to give them numbers to remember you with if you possibly can.

So, why do you want to work for that particular company? A lot of places ask this or something similar. You want to phrase it in a way that doesn't make you a ________ noser but at the same time gets you the job. "I studied the company, and my goals of rising in the organization and your goals of expansion fit well together." If, as an employer, you don't want to move up, I don't really think I want to hire you, I want someone who is going to make my organization money.

Greatest strength

Another likely question is, "Tell me about your greatest strength." Be honest because if you're hired you're going to have to back it up. Understand all the components of the job they are looking to fill. They want you to have one of those skills they are advertising *now* as a strong point. That will be a major plus for you and is another reason why researching a company is so important.

Do not pick something that is not directly related to the job they are advertising; they don't care that you are the neighborhood tennis champion. Take one of the skills needed for the job and turn into it into a positive light. For example, if they are advertising for an electronics engineer or technician, picture some of the skills that you have in regard to their position as your strength. For instance, "I have been fortunate to have a mentor who taught me how to weld stainless steel fences" or "My customer service skills are especially good. I was trained at Disneyland where the guest is always right."

Greatest weakness

They will also want to know about your greatest weakness. That's much harder to answer. None of us likes to admit to a flaw and do not want to talk about it even if we did recognize it.

Again, think about the skills you might need for the job and turn that skill around and make it a weakness you are in control of. For instance, when I answer the question concerning my weakness, I try to be really honest. I say that "I know I am not the most organized person in the world" or "You know sometimes my organizational skills are not the best in the world, but I've found a couple of systems that work for me so that I'm working on being better." What I did was juggle and let them know that I am a work-in-progress and willing to learn to improve myself. Interviewers already know that you're not perfect, so be honest yet turn it into as much a positive as possible.

Many people say they "work too hard" so that's kind of trite (and mostly not believed). On one of the hiring committees I sat on, a young man said he didn't have any weaknesses. Seriously? Get real! Admit to a real weakness and give some thought as to how you could improve that weakness.

Badmouthing

A friend was asked in an interview to describe the worst boss she ever had. This type of question is a red flag question. You *never ever ever ever* want to talk bad about one of your former bosses, Even if your boss was an unfair jerk, talking behind his or her back shows a level of immaturity and a lack of loyalty. You also do not talk negatively about your co-workers for the same reasons.

If they ask that kind of question simply tell them, "Probably I've had the same experience as all of you—I've had great bosses and I've had not-so-great bosses but overall I have really enjoyed the places I've worked." This lets them know that you're not willing to badmouth former colleagues or employers any more than you would speak negatively about them. If one of the hiring committee presses it, I tell them, "I am not comfortable discussing the personalities of my past bosses"—and don't do it.

Oddities

One of the questions sometimes asked even in a standard interview is, "If you could be any animal, what would you choose?" What they are examining is how quickly you think on your feet and how good are your critical thinking skills. One answer I've thought suitable is, "I would be an eagle so that I can soar above the earth." I know it sounds corny but that's the kind of thing they're looking for. "I'm very loyal so I'd select to be a lion because he's the head of a pride." Whatever they ask, it's to examine how you react to immediate situations and your creativity as you are doing so. They might put you into some scenarios that are a bit off the wall.

Off limits (most of the time)

There are certain questions that employers are not supposed to ask. Privacy laws prohibit questions that concern your age, your sexual orientation, your ethnicity, your marital status, and if you have children. Such items are none of their business as it does not affect your working responsibilities. They can ask if you're over 18 (or 21), whatever the requirement is with the position. They can ask if you can provide proof that you are a citizen or that you have a legal right to work in the United States.

Sometimes someone slips up and asks a question that is illegal. There's a couple of schools of thought about this. You have to really think this through yourself. Do I want to answer this question knowing that it's not supposed to be asked? You can go ahead and answer it if you can answer the question with a smile attached ("I'm thirty-one years old"). You can simply state that you are sorry but the question makes you uncomfortable or you can remain silent until the leader of the group hopefully intervenes.

My way is a little more direct; I ask the leader of the interviewers if that question isn't an invasion of privacy. If questions continue in this vein (items that are illegal) you need to ask yourself if the interviewer is unaware of the legality of the issue or pushing the envelope. Either way you might ask yourself if you really want to work for a company that knowingly does illegal interviews.

There may be a gray area. I'm sure that some people in small businesses don't understand that some questions are off-limits. I have read that some of the older generation really do not know that they're not supposed to ask any question they are curious about. Bottom line is, as I said before, you decide if you can answer the prohibited question with genuine comfort.

THE END

At the end of the interview you will be asked if you have questions for them. You say, yes. This demonstrates to them that you're taking an interest in their company and their situation. You always have a question even if it's just to ask what kind of benefits are available.

You do not ask about salary at the interview. If you get a second interview where you are one of the top two or three candidates, they will bring it up probably by asking you what kind of salary you're looking for? There are certain sites with this kind of information, like salary.com, where you can find out what the average salary is for that industry in a particular area of the country. Always keep in mind that certain areas of the country pay high salaries but the cost of living is also high. Salary may not be the only factor in your decision, depending on your goals and ideals.

GRATITUDE

After the interview, thank all individuals you met and shake their hand. In a big organization, they may take you out to lunch after your interview or provide you with a tour of the facility. This gives them further information about you in a casual setting. This is still part of the interview process so treat it as such. The person showing you around will have an opinion on who fits, or does not fit, into the company.

NEXT STEP

Okay, now you are finished with shaking the last person's hand and thanking them for their time. (Remember to thank the receptionist, too, if you exit nearby.) Next thing you do is go back to your car, and drive to the local dollar store so that you can buy some little thank-you cards. Now you're yelling, "What, why would I do that?"

Here's the thing: you want to make people feel good. And you want to make them remember the person the note is from. Your little note should thank them for the interview and add that you enjoyed talking with them. Mention something positive about the business. Put your note in a little envelope with a stamp and drop it in the mailbox.

The alternative course is to send an e-mail. Remember that this is still part of the interview so keep the note and e-mail at the professional level. Your e-mail is an extension of who you are.

My preference is a handwritten card. Everyone does an e-mail and it can get lost in the shuffle. A handwritten note is more personal; however, there's nothing wrong with sending both.

Here's the rule: After you sent an e-mail or a personal note, it is alright to call them to ask when they expect the hiring decision to be made. For example, you say, "This is so-and-so. I interviewed with you on this day at this time." Remember you're not the only person they interviewed (and may be still in the process of interviewing). You need to let them know who you are and that you are just checking in. Mention to whomever you are talking that you enjoyed talking with them and are still interested in the position. This will be a reminder of who you are again. You don't want to become a nuisance so if you haven't heard from them in another week or two, e-mail them to let them know if you are still interested in their company and you hope to hear from them soon.

Personal informal poll

I took an informal poll of my family and friends to see what they had been asked in a standard interview. The most asked question is number one on the list. (The sample size was too small for ranking other questions.)

Standard Questions Asked by Interviewers

- Tell us about yourself.
- What is your biggest strength?
- What is your biggest weakness?
- Why should we hire you?
- What do you bring to the company no one else can?
- Where do you see yourself in five years?
- Why did you leave your last job?
- Why did you apply to this particular business?
- Are you willing to travel?
- If you moved up in the company, are you willing to relocate?
- Are you able to train for a month in another city?

Amazingly many of them were asked the same questions whether they were interviewing for a small, local company or a large organization. Standard questions were asked most frequently, but the most recently employed friends were also asked at least some behavioral questions (covered in the next chapter). I also checked with an online resource, best-job-interview.com, to be sure my personal poll was accurate.

DISCUSSION QUESTIONS

1. What are some issues in answering the question about your strengths and weaknesses?
2. What are some taboos when interviewing? Why are they unacceptable?
3. What questions are off-limits in an interview because of privacy laws?
4. What are some rules as to appropriate dress?

TERMS TO REMEMBER

Privacy	Badmouthing	Thank you
Interrupting	Uniqueness	Question

THINGS TO REMEMBER

- There are no excuses for being late.
- Do not ask about salary at the first interview.
- Never badmouth a former boss or colleague.
- Never lie or exaggerate at an interview; everything will be checked.

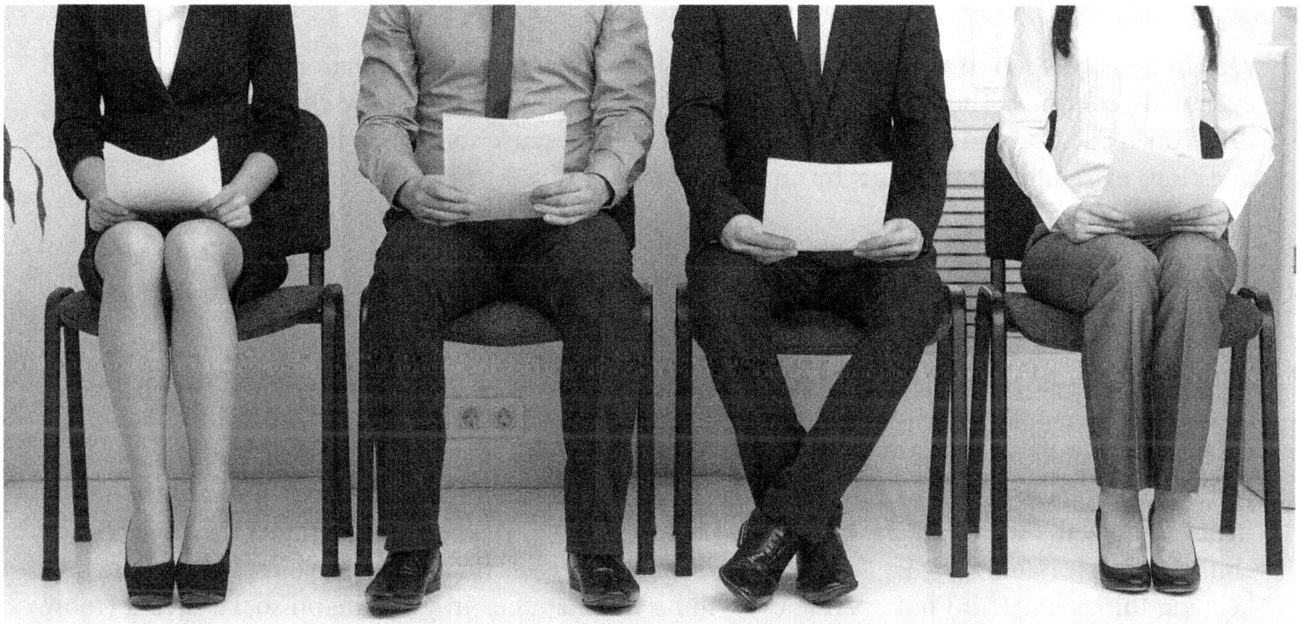

CHAPTER 8

BEHAVIORAL INTERVIEW

As we discussed in the last chapter, the interview is where the big decision will be made—that is, who is the best candidate for this job in this company? All of the same factors apply, from arriving on time, to appropriate dress, to follow-up thank-you letters. If in doubt, reread the last chapter. It is more than likely that all interviews will include some standard questions also. Most employers try to cover as much territory concerning their job hires in the interview process. This is their only shot at choosing the right person also.

It is becoming more and more common for interviewers to ask behavioral-based interview questions. This kind of question requires a concrete, think-on-your feet answer. In the standard interview you've had the time to mull over the possible questions and memorize some possible answers. That is not going to be the case here.

That is not to say you can't prepare for behavioral questions, however. Usually when asked an unfamiliar question, people fall back and depend on their past experiences to answer. Companies who ask behavioral questions are depending on the fact that past behavior will be an indicator of future actions. Whatever your blueprint was in your past performances will carry over into your new employment. If you did the minimum "to get by," then it is probable that you will continue in the same vein in your new job. If you were a leader in your old employment situation, then that, too, will eventually continue. Their thoughts are that people seldom, if ever, truly change. Just by reading this, you are setting yourself apart from other people, because some people don't even know these questions exist and just try to get by on their charm.

SOFT SKILLS

Every employer I have ever asked, from the Idaho Department of Labor to the U.S. Department of Labor, and numerous magazines and books, all say the same thing when asked what they really look for in an employee. Most say they are looking for (drum roll, please...) soft skills. What the heck are soft skills, you ask? They used to be called customer service skills, but it really goes much further than that. It is not only the ability to get along and treat customers well, but also the ability to get along with other workers. It is the ability to get along with the boss, vendors, co-workers; the ability to be pleasant in the workplace, no matter what else is happening in your personal life. It is keeping things quiet and not posting everything that happens in your life on social media (more on this in Chapter 10). Remember these things when they are asking questions and think how you could frame your response to show you have soft skills.

THE REAL YOU

Employers hope that by asking behavioral questions, you will give them some indication of how you think and of your potential behavior in their job. Now they just have to delve deep enough into your character to find the real you. They want to know if you think logically and yet with integrity. They want to know how you react to different situations, especially in the midst of work-related chaos. They especially want to know how you handle difficult people in conflict. They want to know how committed you will be to your new job and how competitive you are and how that relates to team work (both positively and negatively).

DIFFERENT JOBS = DIFFERENT QUESTIONS

Each job you apply for will have different behavioral questions but there is a general trend. The easiest way to prepare yourself for any question is to pretend you are the employer; put yourself in his or her position. Now what do you want an employee to be? You've narrowed the field down through the resume process and your remaining candidates are within the scope of what you advertised. What would you ask a potential employee?

One way would be to ask an organized set of questions delving into how the candidate thinks and then expanding on the same set of questions to dig deeper into the candidates thought processes.

Another way is to ask questions you would expect the candidate to answer based on past experiences and personal attitudes. Many interviews are a combination of these plus several questions from a standard interview.

The absolute best advice: *Practice your answers*! A friend was going before her National Boards for a psychology certification. She asked her husband to think of all the questions possible and he asked a very difficult question regarding how a part of the brain worked if such and so happened. She struggled with the answer but finally felt comfortable with her answer. The exact same question came up during the interview! The more you prepare for the interview, the more confidence you have and the better your response. Without practice her answer would have been incomplete, inept, and she would have been slow in responding.

So, who should you practice with? How about yourself to start out with, in front of a mirror or in the car on the ride home. Say them aloud (who cares what that person in the car next to you thinks of you) as this makes them more real life and pay attention not only to the words but the pitch and inflection of your words. Practice until you are confident in your answers.

Now, say them aloud to your dog, cat, fish, roommate, husband, wife, mother, father, sister, brother, cousin, or anyone else you can get to sit down with you (after a while, if you are doing this right, people will start to avoid you).

Your customer service skills

Say you are applying for an entry-level job at Staples which will eventually lead toward mid-management and your own store. If you were the employer, what do you need to know? Probably the applicants' customer service skills (you have their resumes so you know their electronic and computer skills), so one of the questions you might ask them is how they would handle a customer who kept complaining about the lack of the choice of paper products—something you do not have any control of? Your response might go something like, "I'm so sorry, sir, we didn't have the paper you wanted. We do have a more extensive selection in our catalogue, however. Please come this way, and I'll show you some other choices." You would also tell the interviewer that the customer is always right and that you would answer the customer with a genuine smile and show courtesy.

This would be okay, but it is kind of generic. When I was working at Disneyland, we had some of the best customer service training in the world. They taught us that the customer is always right and to do everything in your power to make sure he or she is happy. Did you catch that? Everything in your power...I once had to deliver two televisions from Bozeman, Montana, to Yellowstone National Park (2½ hours each way) in the middle of winter. You know what, I did it and the person gave me a $100 tip. That is customer service! I am sure you have some stories from your experiences. Dust them off and have them ready for your interviews.

Different approaches

In a behavioral interview there are no absolute right and absolute wrong answers; as in most things in life it depends on the situation. You have no idea what the employer is looking for. Several years ago, I interviewed for a summer job at the same time that a friend was also applying. I knew that his experience and skill set was more extensive than my own but I thought what the heck, it will give me better interviewing familiarity. I ended up with the job. Later I found out that my background of growing up in a small minority town which I considered "home" had been the deciding factor.

The boss later said that skills were important but understanding the people I would work with was essential. Be honest with your interviewer. And then with yourself.

MY INFORMAL POLL

From my informal poll of family and friends, I found that the most common question asked in a behavioral interview forum was:

"What is an example of how you handled a situation when a co-worker was making your job difficult?"

No absolutes and no easy answers here. It depends on the person, his or her diverse background, and each level of management. Give an honest evaluation. Things like talking to your superior, becoming more knowledgeable about the person, and working with that person on a project are all good ways to handle a situation but you must do your own. A secretary was being an absolute witch to work with (notice I didn't use the other word). After talking to the supervisor, it was revealed that her breast cancer was no longer in remission and she wanted it kept secret. It was a lot easier to cut her some slack and try to help her.

"Would you go into more detail please? If that hadn't worked, what was your plan B?"

Get creative; there are a multitude of things that could be done. Talk to other people if you run out of ideas. Especially talk to older adults with lots of work experiences as they may have encountered the problems before. Maybe they can give you ideas or you can use some of their experiences as examples. I still remember my grandfather telling me the line, "An honest day's work for an honest day's pay," although he must have told it to me when I was only a youngster.

The second most common question was:

"Dishonesty is common in business. Tell me about a time when you saw this occur and what you did."

This hits that integrity bar. Did you report the missing box of paper clips? How about the missing chair? How large an item would you ignore? See, a slippery slope but a question that is often asked, especially in retail as stealing among staff is a million-dollar loss for some companies. So, you see your friend walk out the door with some merchandise. Do you call him on it? Do you ignore her? Do you listen when he tells you to be cool? Is being popular with that friend worth your own job? This is a hard question and I suggest you think about it.

Almost everyone polled had a version of this one:

"Tell me about a time when you did not agree with your boss's decision and what you did."

This again will depend on the situation. Most of the time if it's not illegal, immoral, or fattening, we say it's his or her company. However, many of us did give our opinions to the boss. This has to be done in the right way, of course. You cannot just tell the boss he or she is wrong. Like I always tell my students, you can argue with me all you want, but you better be able to back it up. This means if you argue with the boss or think your way of doing something is better, then you better be able to back up those words. Think of some examples that show this. Now, phrase them in a way so you don't look or sound like you are being a smart ____. That is what you need to answer this question.

Another common question was:

> *"You have worked at several places of employment. How have you handled when the job expectations are unrealistic? Please go into detail."*

Be honest, please. Some of the people I polled had expected to rise faster in the company; they went to their bosses and discussed those feelings. After that, they made the decision to stay or look for something with more fulfillment. One person said that he had not realized that the computer company he worked for did not allow time for a social life with his new wife. He talked to his boss and they compromised. Confession: when I was managing a popular retail store, I often left more work for the night crew than they could possibly do in one night. I knew they could either do part of the work well or do all of the work shoddily. Their response to this showed me their work ethic.

So, as an employer, what answer would I want to hear to this question? I would want them to be honest with me but I would want them to try first. If they found they really couldn't handle their workload, they needed to come and talk to me and let me know. Perhaps, like my scenario, I just want to see if they do half the work well or if they fold under the pressure. Regardless, I want them to act like adults and not whine and complain all the time but to go through the channels to see how they are as workers. Now, come up with some stories of your own.

Another question:

> *"We are a fast-paced company. Tell me about a time in your past employment when you have had to be both flexible and rushed."*

See the question above, too. For hyperactive me and many of my family members, busy is best. Flexible is easy—having patience, not so much. Think of a past scenario that shows you in a good light, though. I would always want it be busy when I was working in retail. Otherwise it was boring. As much as I hated the busy holidays, it made the time fly by. My brother-in-law is a policeman in a major U.S. city. He prefers to work the graveyard shift in the worst area of the city. Why? Because time flies by. I enjoy working and teaching a lot of classes. Why, same answer, because time flies by.

Another:

> *"Tell me about a time when you've had a boss who knew less about the job than you did and how you coped with it."*

Remember that time when your patience was a problem? This is where you show it. Let's say you have been working a job for a while, and that promotion you were hoping for goes to someone else they just hired. Or worse, to one of the boss's relatives. They want you to train the new hire. So, what do you do? Are you gracious and train the person well? Or do you have a bad attitude and eventually quit? This answer tells a lot about you. It could say you are a good employee and willing to do what is best for the company. Or it could say you are a little kid who is upset and let it get to you and affect your job.

I have actually had this happen several times. Of course I was upset. But I got over it quickly and went on with my job. The way I looked at it in most situations was they must have had a reason for what they did. So I just worked harder. However, another time it became apparent they had no intention of promoting me. When I asked them about it, the boss said," I can't afford to promote you, you're too good at your present job." I put in my two weeks shortly after that. I didn't burn my bridges and tell them off, but boy did I want to. Sometimes the person will be incompetent and try to get you to do all the work or try to take credit for someone else's work. What do you do? Do your best and let the others bury themselves. They always do.

Got the idea?

Here are some other common ones for management:

"Give me an example of when you had to discipline an employee."

So, this is where you put how mean you are, right? NO. How about where you tell the story about so and so? "This is one of the hardest things a manager has to do..." Nope that was taken by the movie *Bull Durham* when Kevin Costner was let go by his baseball team. No, this is where they want one of your actual experiences to come into play. What if you have never had to do this? Tell them so, because honesty is always best.

I have had to discipline several employees over the years. The best way to do it I have found is to just be honest. State the facts, and let them know if they broke a rule, and tell them the punishment. No beating around the bush. I always hated being on the receiving end of that. Be prepared for a reaction, and above all, handle yourself like an adult.

"Tell me about a time you had to fire someone."

This one is even worse than disciplining someone. How do you tell workers they are fired? I always started the process in the same way. First, I let them know what rules they had broken and that I was letting them go as a result. Again, there is almost always a reaction. I have seen everything from tears to asking me to step outside to talk about it. The trick is not to react and let them get it out. Afterwards, most come to understand what they did was wrong and accept it.

"How do you handle stress in the workplace? In your personal life?"

Without going into a whole chapter on stress, what are some of your outlets? What do you like to do when you have spare time? Do you work out? Read? Ride a motorcycle? Make doll clothes? The answers will vary but your answers should be something to let them know you are not going to overstress yourself and freak out. Everyone needs a way to release stress.

Describe the most challenging project you've had to carry out."

This is a good one to let them know about your skills. You want them to think about you in a positive light and that you have the skills they are looking for. You might want to think along the lines of something you did in which you can put numbers to—remember, people can easily recall numbers.

One of my favorites is to tell about the time one of my former bosses moved up to area supervisor and I took over his position. It was a sales management position and he was a high-pressure salesperson. I hated that role. So, while the company pushed the high-pressure sales aspect, I used a friendlier approach. Long story short, I consistently beat his sales by over 9% every week. He stopped asking for the high pressure and began watching how I was doing it.

> *"Decision-making skills are an important aspect of this job. Tell me about your thought processes when you have had to make a controversial decision."*

What they are looking for here is your thought process. They want to see how you think critically. In order to do this, you need to first get all of the information, choose the best one, and then make a good decision from it. This is not always easy to do. We all come with preconceived notions of what should be done.

When I answer this question, I usually go back to when I was teaching high school. I had a decision to make about a student who was considered trouble by a lot of the members of the school. I was running an advanced entrepreneurship and marketing class and the class would have to do some traveling, including overnight travel. I talked to some of his former teachers, the assistant principal, and also met with his parents. He really wanted to be in the class. After talking to all the other parties, I concluded by talking to him. I was honest with him and told him I had reservations about it. He said he just wanted a chance, if he screwed up, I could kick him out. Long story short, he was challenging at times, but he was also part of a team that placed third in the country at a competition in San Diego. He later went on to college, and I lost track of him. I should look him up on Facebook and see what happened to him.

Employers' wants

Again, what the employers who use the behavioral interview want is

- To check your customer service skills
- To see if you use have superior decision-making skills
- To know if you are team player
- To find out if you are a potential loyal employee
- To see if you get along with people both above you and below you
- To see if you are capable of working with diverse populations
- To know if you have a life outside work

Research has shown that a well-rounded person makes the best employee with better production and staying power.

PHONE INTERVIEWS

Phone interviews are to screen likely candidates before an interview. Usually phone interviews are done when there is a distance between the employer and interviewee. This cuts down on travel and is a convenient source of information gathering. Phone interviews narrow the field to the few candidates who are possible good fits for the company's goals and needs. Most phone interviews are similar to the standard interview we talked about in the last chapter.

Since nonverbal communication plays a part in behavioral interviews, the phone interview is more about your resume, job skills, and experience. Only a few people in my informal poll had ever participated in a phone interview as it is usually a prelude to offering a face-to-face meeting or interview.

The first question we were all asked was:

"Why are you looking for new employment?"

This should be answered in a way that doesn't denigrate your present employer but let your potential new employer know you are looking to move up. A good answer would be, "While I am presently employed, it is not giving me the chances for promotion or it doesn't challenge me in a way I feel I need to be challenged." This lets them know you are serious about personal growth.

"What are your short-term goals? What about long-term aspirations?"

This is the equivalent of where you want to be in five or ten years. Please, whatever you do, don't answer, "In five years I want to be in your job." This is seen as threatening to many people who may be insecure in their position. Rather, "I want to be given the opportunity to move up and hopefully in five years that will have become a reality." As for ten years, even if you want to do it, don't tell them you eventually want to start your own business. It takes a lot of money to develop an employee, and no employer wants to hear that you are simply using them as a stepping stone.

"How competent are you in MOUS applications?"

This question is asking how competent you are on a computer. A MOUS certification indicates you are an expert at Microsoft Office. Please don't lie and say you are if you are not. Better to tell them you are good but not an expert if you aren't. I always appreciate honesty.

"Are you willing to move to a new location?"

Think about this one. If you aren't willing, say so. If you have a family that wants to stay in a certain area for the good schools or if you don't want to be separated from them, say so. However, if you are ready and willing to try new things and places, by all means let them know.

"What is your salary now?"

This one is tricky. You need to have an idea of the salary they are offering so you have something to compare it to. If your present salary is good, but you want the new position because it offers better promotions or lets you work in your career field, that works well for an answer.

"Why do you want this particular job with this particular company?"

This is where your research comes in. You should be able to tell them why their company interests you. Don't you dare say the money! Money is nice but the money is only a means to an end. What should really interest you is what you will be doing for the company. If they have an exciting project that you want to be part of, let them know. It also lets them know you did your homework.

"Do you have questions for us that were not addressed in the interview?"

YOU WILL HAVE QUESTIONS! This is where you can pull out your list from your research and impress them. Please have questions as it shows that you have done your homework and that you are interested. (There is always something that you want to know; even if it's about the community.)

PITFALLS

Here is an example from a friend: "The dot.com company I was working for folded; dang. I loved that job. I moved to an area where I grew up and had a lot of networking resources. I heard about an accounting job which I qualified for due to some college-required courses. I applied and was interviewed. The HR interviewer told me thank you but that I was overqualified, and if they hired me, they were afraid I would move on and they would be in the same place they are now—looking for an employee. I had to smile and thank him for the interview because he was right! The first decent offer I would receive I would be so gone! I would have wasted that company's time and resources."

Some other things to think about…If you are asked if you can travel, have your answer ready. Many companies require some travel but many are also flexible about the issue. Ask if they are talking about travelling two weeks every month or one week every three months? Then be candid. If it's not possible for you due to your other responsibilities, tell them why. It may not even be a deal-breaker.

There are a ton of free websites with examples of phone, standard, and behavioral interview questions. Use them! The more you are prepared the better your interview; knowledge really is power. The questions won't be exactly the same but they will be in the same tone and pattern. You will also have more confidence when you feel more comfortable in a situation. That confidence will tend to make you more enthusiastic with your answers and your demeanor.

CODE OF CONDUCT

One last thing for this chapter. Peter Luongo, author of "10 Truths About Leadership—It's Not Just About Winning" has a story of The Berry Company and its refocusing on a code of conduct-oriented behavior-driven model. This is certainly not a new concept but a valuable one nonetheless.

The basic tenant of this model is a problem-solving program called Character Counts taught in many schools throughout the country. It is another useful tool which teaches students strategies for life skills in the developmental years of elementary and high school.

If you were fortunate enough to have a Character Counts program at your elementary or high school, their six pillars are quite literally what most employers are looking for. If you didn't, those life skills are:

Trustworthiness

Be honest • Don't deceive, cheat, or steal • Be reliable—do what you say you'll do • Have the courage to do the right thing • Build a good reputation • Be loyal—stand by your family, friends, and country

Respect

Treat others with respect; follow the Golden Rule • Be tolerant of differences • Use good manners, not bad language • Be considerate of the feelings of others • Don't threaten, hit, or hurt anyone • Deal peacefully with anger, insults, and disagreements

Responsibility

Do what you are supposed to do • Persevere: keep on trying! • Always do your best • Use self-control • Be self-disciplined • Think before you act—consider the consequences • Be accountable for your choices

Fairness

Play by the rules • Take turns and share • Be open-minded; listen to others • Don't take advantage of others • Don't blame others carelessly

Caring

Be kind • Be compassionate and show you care • Express gratitude • Forgive others • Help people in need

Citizenship

Do your share to make your school and community better • Cooperate • Get involved in community affairs • Stay informed; vote • Be a good neighbor • Obey laws and rules • Respect authority • Protect the environment

DISCUSSION QUESTIONS

1. Why would an employer use a behavioral interview to look for job skills?
2. What are the merits of the behavioral interview as opposed to the standard interview from the standpoint of the employer? Of the interviewee?
3. What kind of information is gained through a phone interview?
4. Discuss essential customer service skills.

TERMS TO REMEMBER

Respect	Citizenship	Trustworthiness
Fairness	Responsibility	Caring

THINGS TO REMEMBER

- There are no absolutes and no easy way out.
- Practice possible answers.
- Knowledge is power.
- Honesty equals integrity.

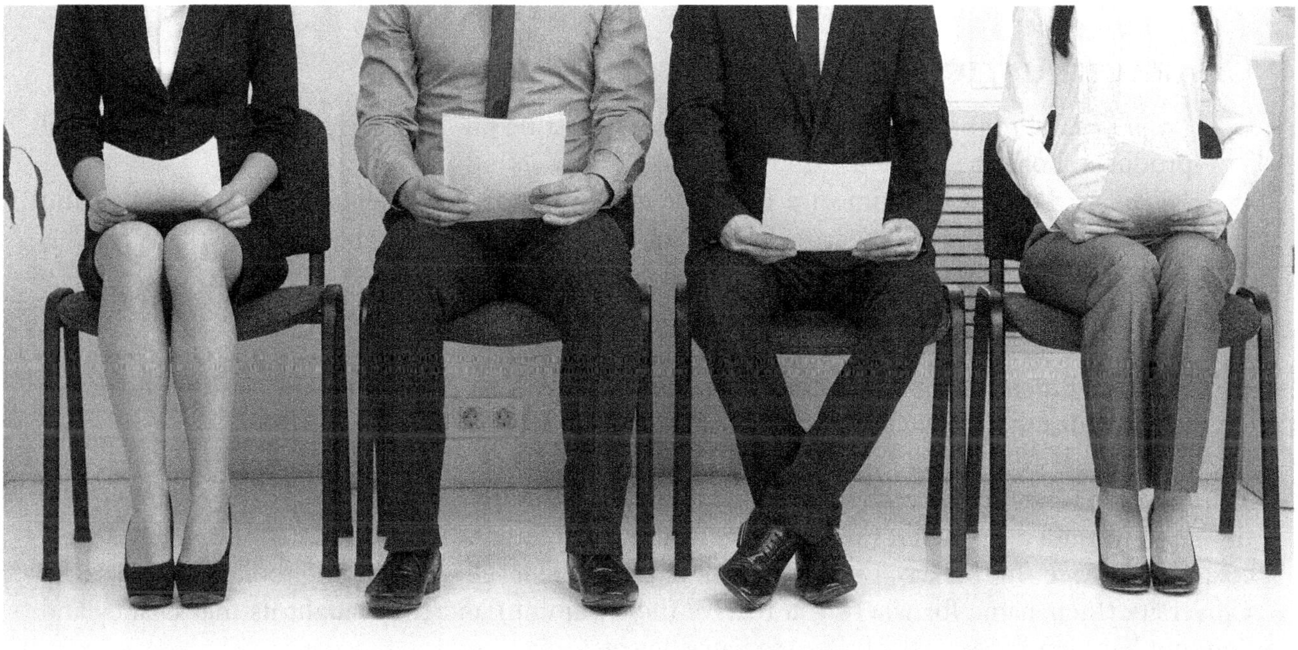

CHAPTER 9

HOW TO KEEP THE JOB

OK, you got the job, now what? First of all, congratulations, the job market is rapidly improving but it is still a tough thing to do. In this chapter, we will explore a few things that happen in workplaces and how to deal with them.

CUSTOMER SERVICE

No matter what job you go into, you will have to deal with someone else. My department chair, when speaking to one of my classes, challenged the class to name a job where you never have to deal with anyone else. As expected, no one could. Even the hermit who lives up in the mountains has to come down to get coffee or to sell his wares. A computer programmer who works at home is programming for someone. We all have others we have to work with in our lives. Getting along with them is another matter.

So what exactly is customer service? The ACA Group sums up what the meaning of customer service is beautifully: "Customer service (is) the ability of an organization to constantly and consistently exceed the customer's expectations." In other words, customer service is meeting the needs and desires of any customer.

Characteristics of Good Customer Service

- *Promptness:* Promises for delivery of products must be on time. Delays and cancellations of products should be avoided.
- *Politeness:* Politeness is almost a lost art. Saying "hello," "good afternoon, madam/sir," and "thank you very much" is part of good customer service. For any business, a "thank you" is appropriate whether the customer makes a purchase or not.
- *Professionalism:* All customers should be treated professionally. Using this characteristic of good customer service shows customers that you really care about them.
- *Personalization:* Using the customer's name is very effective in producing loyalty. Customers like the idea that retailers know them on a personal level (McKinney, 2015).

Years ago, after I graduated high school, I worked for Disneyland. Before you ask the obvious question, no I was not a character; I worked in one of the restaurants. There I learned the value of great customer service. To this day, I strive to achieve this same level. Our training took place at Disney University (their name for where you receive their training) and they taught us that Disneyland does not have employees, they have associates. Disneyland does not have customers, they have guests. These guests are the lifeblood of everything they do. The rule is not, as some people say, to give customers anything they want. It is not even the old saying that the customer is always right. Their motto is the guest is always right, provided you can accomplish making that guest happy. This leaves room to do almost anything within reason to accommodate the guest.

Featureflash/Shutterstock, Inc.

This seems like a good way to do things. If we do our utmost to keep our customers happy, we can usually keep them as customers. One of the realities of customer service is that without those customers, you will not have a business. Sure, businesses are in business to make a profit, but without making those customers happy, you will not be in business very long. Customers are the lifeblood of any business or nonprofit, whether it be a bank, retail store, school, or other government entity. Without those customers, YOU WILL NOT HAVE A JOB OR BUSINESS.

MOTIVATION

"Motivated employees work harder, produce higher quality and greater quantities of work, are more likely to engage in organizational citizenship behaviors, and are less likely to leave the organization in search of more fulfilling opportunities" (Sadri and Bowen, 2011). We all need to be motivated to do our best work. There is a deep sense of satisfaction in a job well done. Most people want to do a good job.

GROUPS

marekuliasz/Shutterstock, Inc.

"Never doubt that a small group of thoughtful, committed people can change the world. Indeed, it is the only thing that ever has." —Margaret Mead

Most people do not like to work in groups in the workplace. For most, the group they are in seems to always have one or two people who do most of the work, while the others do nothing but still get all the credit. As I said in an earlier chapter, suck it up, Buttercup. The fact of life in most workplaces is that you are going to have to work in groups.

Let's examine some of the dynamics of working in a group. Let's start with group formation. Every group goes through stages of formation and ultimately breakup. Consider the five steps of Tuckman's linear model of group development:

Forming: Members come together, learn about each other, and determine the purpose of the group.
Storming: Members engage in more direct communication and get to know each other. Conflicts between group members will often arise during this stage.
Norming: Members establish spoken or unspoken rules about how they communicate and work. Status, rank, and roles in the group are established.
Performing: Members fulfill their purpose and reach their goal.
Adjourning: Members leave the group.

Most workplaces work together to achieve the highest level of production. This means they will often work in teams. Often, that means you will be working with others you may not feel comfortable around. Maybe it is because you do not know them, or because they are from a completely different skill set from you. They may be a different ethnicity from you or from a different part of the world. They may speak a different language or have an accent. Regardless, you will still have to work with them.

TEAM BUILDING

Teams and groups alike go through different stages. According to Tuckman's linear model of group development, teams go through the same stages of forming, storming, norming, performing, and adjourning. Not all teams or groups will reach each stage. Some will get stuck in one stage while others will have to relive a stage as they go backwards instead of forward in their development. In each stage, there are certain activities. In each stage, I'll describe the activities and give an example.

Forming is the beginning stage. In this stage, people are getting to know each other, personal relations are formed through the dependence on the group. Group members rely on safe, patterned behavior and look to the group leader for guidance and direction. Group members have a desire for acceptance by the group and a need to know that the group is safe. They set about gathering impressions and data about the similarities and differences among them and forming preferences for future subgrouping. Rules of behavior seem to be to keep things simple and to avoid controversy. Serious topics and feelings are avoided. The major task functions also concern orientation. Members attempt to become oriented to the tasks as well as to one another. Discussion centers around defining the scope of the task, how to approach it, and similar concerns. To grow from this stage to the next, each member must relinquish the comfort of nonthreatening topics and risk the possibility of conflict.

For this stage, imagine you are on sports team, or a member of a club. The team or club has just been formed from names pulled out of a hat. That is what this stage is like. The people may or may not know each other. The personalities have not come out and everyone is pretty nice to each other while getting to know their roles in the group. Leaders may start to see who their rivals for leadership would be but no steps are taken to try and get that leadership. The people who are normally in the background will start to drift that way.

Storming is the next stage, which is characterized by competition and conflict in the personal-relations dimension. As the group members attempt to organize for the task, conflict inevitably results in their personal relations. Individuals have to bend and mold their feelings, ideas, attitudes, and beliefs to suit the group organization. Because of "fear of exposure" or "fear of failure," there will be an increased desire for structural clarification and commitment. Although conflicts may or may not surface as group issues, they do exist. Questions will arise about who is going to be responsible for what, what the rules are, what the reward system is, and what criteria for evaluation are. These reflect conflicts over leadership, structure, power, and authority. There may be wide swings in members' behavior based on emerging issues of competition and hostilities. Because of the discomfort generated during this stage, some members may remain completely silent while others attempt to dominate.

In order to progress to the next stage, group members must move from a "testing and proving" mentality to a problem-solving mentality. The most important trait in helping groups to move on to the next stage seems to be the ability to listen.

In this stage, our fledging team or club is starting to develop a personality. The leaders emerge and a competition for leadership will emerge. If there is no leader, a leader will be thrust forward by the group. Other personality traits will emerge as people get more comfortable with each other. The wallflowers will retreat into the background as stronger personalities take over. There will be some infighting going on and the members will try and assert themselves in their area of expertise.

Norming involves interpersonal relations characterized by cohesion. Group members are engaged in active acknowledgment of all members' contributions, community building and maintenance, and solving of group issues. Members are willing to change their preconceived ideas or opinions on the basis of facts presented by other members, and they actively ask questions of one another. Leadership is shared, and cliques dissolve. When members begin to know and identify with one another, the level of trust in their personal relations contributes to the development of group cohesion. It is during this stage of development (assuming the group gets this far) that people begin to experience a sense of group belonging and a feeling of relief as a result of resolving interpersonal conflicts. The major task function of this third stage is the data flow between group members: They share feelings and ideas, solicit and give feedback to one another, and explore actions related to the task. Creativity is high. If this stage of data flow and cohesion is attained by the group members, their interactions are characterized by openness and sharing of information on both a personal and task level. They feel good about being part of an effective group.

Our little team or club has gotten over the rough patch and is now functioning fairly well. The leader or leaders have resolved their differences for the most part and everyone has fallen into their roles. A secretary or recorder is taking the notes and distributing them out to members. A person's expertise is recognized and each member gets into the role he/she has been given.

Performing is not reached by all groups. If group members are able to evolve to this fourth stage, their capacity, range, and depth of personal relations expand to true interdependence. In this stage, people can work independently, in subgroups, or as a total unit with equal facility. Their roles and authorities dynamically adjust to the changing needs of the group and individuals. This stage is marked by interdependence in personal relations and problem solving in the realm of task functions. By now, the group should be most productive. Individual members have become self-assuring, and the need for group approval is past. Members are both highly task oriented and highly people oriented. There is unity: group identity is complete, group morale is high, and group loyalty is intense. The task function becomes genuine problem solving, leading toward optimal solutions and optimum group development. There is support for experimentation in solving problems and an emphasis on achievement. The overall goal is productivity through problem solving and work.

Remember, not all groups will reach this stage. Now in regards to our little team or club, this is the stage most people dream of. The team is operating on high efficiency. All of the parts are working in synchronicity or seamless. It is a well-run machine with everyone having fit into their roles and everyone knows what everyone else is doing.

Adjourning, Tuckman's final stage, involves the termination of task behaviors and disengagement from relationships. A planned conclusion usually includes recognition for participation and achievement and an opportunity for members to say personal goodbyes. Concluding a group can create some apprehension—in effect, a minor crisis. The termination of the group is a regressive movement from giving up control to giving up inclusion in the group. The most effective interventions in this stage are those that facilitate task termination and the disengagement process.

In this stage, our group is split. Either one or several members leave the group. This causes the group to regress. The group may go all the way back to forming or to storming as new members are inserted or if no new members are added then others have to pick up the slack in the group, doing the work that is now left to others.

Do you recognize some of these dynamics in groups you have worked in? I know I have worked with groups in these various stages. The trick is being honest enough with yourself and the group to know what stage you are in at that moment in time.

mast3r/Shutterstock, Inc.

GROUP ROLES

As in life, everyone has roles we play. Shakespeare wrote, "All the world's a stage" and it still remains true. We all have roles we play in groups, also. As you can see from the tables, some of these roles are positive, some are negative. Also, a person can assume more than one role within the group.

Positive Roles	
Initiator-coordinator	Suggests new ideas or new ways of looking at the problem
Elaborator	Builds on ideas and provides examples
Coordinator	Brings ideas, information, and suggestions together
Evaluator-critic	Evaluates ideas and provides constructive criticism
Recorder	Records ideas, examples, suggestions, and critiques

Negative Roles	
Dominator	Dominates discussion, not allowing others to take their turn
Recognition seeker	Relates discussion to their accomplishments; seeks attention
Special-interest pleader	Relates discussion to special interest or personal agenda
Blocker	Blocks attempts at consensus consistently
Joker or clown	Seeks attention through humor and distracts group members

MEETINGS

Rawpixel/Shutterstock, Inc.

Ah yes, meetings, everyone's favorite thing to spend half a day sitting in. There are ways to make them more efficient though. First, have an agenda. Send it out in advance, if this is not possible, print out copies. Next, stick to the agenda; don't let anyone lead the meeting off on a tangent. This will make for longer meetings.

Next, when discussing things, use the old military way. Have the most junior persons in the room go first. This lets them speak and not just give a rubber stamp to the most senior people in the room. Finally, let everyone know they don't have to chime in on every single thing. In a lot of meetings I have been to, what could have been accomplished in 15 minutes takes 2 hours because everyone feels they need to talk, probably to justify their existence. This is where having an agenda comes in—with an agenda, you can push a little bit, letting everyone know you need to get through it. The world is a stage and a meeting is a performance, the same as an interview or speech presentation. Each member has a part to perform and all should be aware of their roles and responsibilities prior to the meeting. A clearly defined agenda can be a productive tool for this effort.

People may know each other by role or title but may not be familiar with each other. Brief introductions can serve to establish identity, credibility, and help the group transition to performance. The purpose of the meeting should be clearly stated, and if there are rules or guidelines that require a specific protocol, they should be introduced.

Mary Ellen Guffey provides this useful participant checklist:

- Arrive on time and stay until the meeting adjourns (unless there are prior arrangements).
- Leave the meeting only for established breaks or emergencies.
- Be prepared and have everything you need on hand.
- Turn off cell phones and personal digital assistants.
- Follow the established protocol for turn taking.
- Respect time limits.
- Demonstrate professionalism in your verbal and nonverbal interactions.
- Communicate interest and stay engaged in the discussion.
- Avoid tangents and side discussions.
- Respect space and don't place your notebook or papers all around you.
- Clean up after yourself.
- Engage in polite conversation after the conclusion.

In short, conduct the meeting; don't let it get away from you.

Bloomua/Shutterstock, Inc.

Following are tips for using technology in the workplace:

1. Your Facebook page. This also includes the other social media sites, LinkedIn, Google +, Pinterest, Twitter, and whatever other one you use. Remember you are at work, some companies have Acceptable Use Policies (AUPs), in which you agree whatever you put on your computer at work is their intellectual property. This means

anything you post, e-mail, or tweet, they have the right to see and ask you about. The safer bet is just to wait until you are home to do any of these things.

2. Cameras, smile, you are probably on camera. Studies have shown we are on camera from 100 to 2,000 times a day. Most of these are security cameras are at places like the ATM when you get money out. Most companies are now using some form of security cameras. This means if you try to do something stupid at work, you are liable to get caught doing it.
3. Working from home: Some companies will allow employees to work from home fairly often. Just remember, this is not an excuse to do nothing all day. Most networks can tell when you are logged in and when there is someone using them. Also, be careful how you dress. A friend was working from home and chatting online with her boss, what she didn't know was the webcam on her laptop was active and she didn't understand enough about Skype to know her boss could see her in her pajamas and no makeup. Needless to say, she was embarrassed.

DISCUSSION QUESTION

1. What are some of the characteristics of good customer service?

TERMS TO REMEMBER

Motivation   Dominator   Groups

THINGS TO REMEMBER

- Without customer service there are no customers.
- All people in a group/team have roles they play.
- All people have to interact with someone sometime.

REFERENCES

Beene, K., and P. Sheats. (1948). Functional roles of group members. *Journal of Social Issues, 37*, 41–49.

McKinney 2015

Sadri, G., and R. C. Bowen, R.C. (2011). Meeting employee requirements. Maslow's hierarchy of needs is still a reliable guide to motivating staff. *Industrial Engineer, 43*(10), 44.

Tuckman, B. (1965). Developmental sequence in small groups. *Psychological Bulletin, 63*, 384–99.

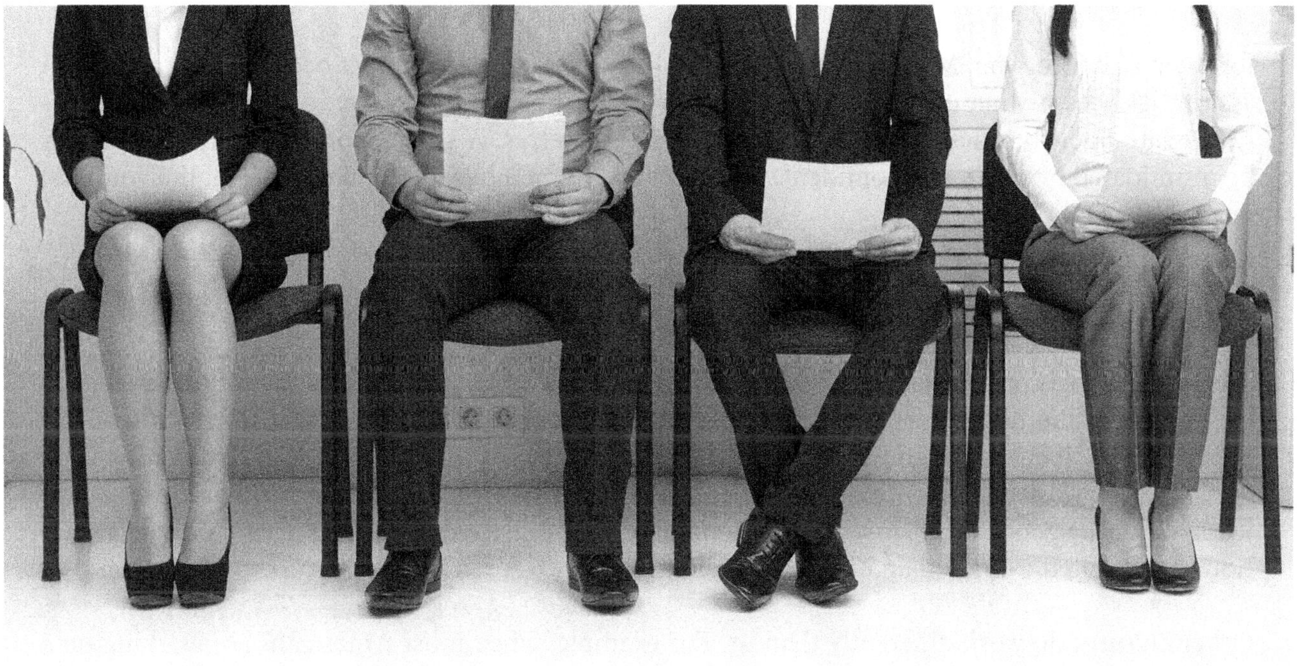

CHAPTER 10

DIVERSITY, ETHICS, AND LEADERSHIP

DIVERSITY AND MULTICULTURALISM

Chances are, depending on the size of your workplace, you will be working with people from a wide variety of backgrounds. In our rapidly expanding world and global marketplace, this will become the new normal. So, what difference does it make what culture or ethnicity someone is? The answer is, maybe it shouldn't but it does. Different ethnicities and cultures will naturally have different habits and customs and this difference shows up in the workplace in a variety of ways. This includes the way they interact with colleagues, how they dress, and their reactions in the workplace. In today's ever changing economy, working successfully with a variety of people is essential.

A FEW RULES

A few rules make life easier. First, don't judge—you haven't walked a mile in their moccasins. Their culture is different than yours, not inferior or superior but different. Second, do your homework. Find out about their country, their taboos, what's important to them. And third, listen to them. Encourage them to talk about how things are done in their country; it will allow you to talk about the differences and possible conflicts you both may encounter. Understanding you may be as difficult for them as it is for you. Make questioning a two-way street. When conflict occurs, and it will, don't assume it's because they are different. It may be because they think they have a better idea. And lastly, provide opportunities for everyone to express themselves. A shy person from any culture may be intimidated by older, self-confident, verbal adults. Remember the military style of the youngest or new hires talk first.

AREAS OF CONFLICT

The biggest areas of conflict caused by a lack of cultural understanding are communication, our lack of understanding others' behaviors, and in foreseeing how their behavior affects others. We expect others to be like us and are baffled when they're not. It can make our jobs frustrating if we don't learn to work effectively in diverse group settings. It's important that the leaders of the groups learn about the people in their sections. Men raised in India, for example, have very different reactions to educated women than men from Columbia, South America.

Other cultures do work differently than us. For example, when most Americans are working on a project, we expect a certain amount of chaos involved with people interrupting with new, terrific ideas. My friend raised in Japan is appalled at the "lack of courtesy" and says he is much more comfortable in a traditional management style of top down. (I'm always intrigued by how he would have managed in our dot.com era of bedlam.)

"Ready for your first lesson in conflict resolution?"

Cartoonresource/Shutterstock, Inc.

Another area which I personally was confronted with is the lack of time management which permeates some cultures. Raised in a small town with time limits on activities I was taken aback by the lack of punctuality when I worked with students and parents from Latin American countries. If they didn't show up at a scheduled meeting it wasn't because of disrespect but one of inconvenience. To them time was plentiful. I had to rethink their cultural values and try to come up with a compromise which would work for my schedule—having the student call my cell phone when there was a delay, for example. Students, too, had to learn that when Mrs. So and So said an assignment was due on Friday, she didn't mean a week from next Tuesday. In the Native American world, there is Anglo time and Native American time. Anglo time has a clock when things start; Native American time starts when everything is ready. 'Nuff said.

An area which is always in flux is "The boss is always right because she's the boss" or "I can question the boss's decision if I don't think he's right." This again boils down to culture and backgrounds. What's comfortable for me with my personality and values may not be comfortable with the person from Cambodia. The United States has always valued individualism—many parts of our laws are based on their protection. However, many Asian cultures base their values on working well within a set parameter and feel being loyal to a company is the correct method for them.

NONVERBAL COMMUNICATION

Sangoiri/Shutterstock, Inc.

Nonverbal communication is where culture clashes show up quickly. Body language, something all cultures use in one way or another, is a good example. According to general consensus, about 80% to 90% of our communication takes place through nonverbal communication. Now to my point: what is common in one culture is NOT universal. In general, most of your colleagues will follow a modified form of their culture and yours; probably a short brief handshake. I've included some facts of other cultural differences for your information.

Shaking hands

In America, the cultural gesture of shaking hands upon greeting is considered the norm when introductions are made. In fact in America, to refuse a handshake is considered a rude gesture. The firmness of the handshake is often material for a joke by television punsters. You know, the two men squeezing each other's hands in a death grip; something that is verboten in all cultures. The American handshake between men is one that is firm and brief with eye contact; with women it is initiated or not by the woman.

In many cultures, for example Asian countries and even most Native American tribes, the handshake between men is a brief contact. With women it may be a touching of the hand or a nod of the head. Anything else would be an uncomfortable encounter. For many traditional Native American men and women living on reservations (and sometimes off reservations) the touching of the palm of the hands is passing your spirit from one person to another. I rather like that.

A-OK

The OK hand gesture in America and England is quite popular and considered a general gesture that denotes an agreement of sentiment. This gesture in Brazil is the equivalent of using your middle finger as a gesture here in America. The OK hand gesture is also taken as an insult in Austria, France, and in most of Latin America.

Thumbs up

The thumbs-up gesture can be an equivalent to the OK gesture and is widely used within America and England. Once again, though, in a large amount of cultures around the globe giving a thumbs-up gesture is an insult. According to Joel Sherzer, a linguistic anthropologist, using the thumbs-up gesture anywhere in the Americas excluding the United States is a horrible idea. Using this gesture can be denoted as a sexual insult and correlates to the middle-finger meaning in the United States.

This is just a small sampling of how simple body language gestures can be interpreted in different cultures. If you do intend to travel abroad the best course of action is to take the time to understand the culture of the country you are going visiting. You may also want to keep your body language in check, to avoid offending anyone until you get the chance to observe their culture better. Human consideration can be the best body language tool you have.

The majority of conscious body language is conducted through hand signals, but there are a lot of gestures involving head movements and facial expressions, too. Gestures such as bowing, cheek kissing, and nodding carry various meanings in different cultures. What does your body language say to others?

Bowing

One of the most important head movements used in body language is bowing. According to culture and custom, the bow signifies different things and is executed in different ways.

Bowing has the most ample meaning in East Asia, particularly in Japan. The meaning varies depending on the way the bow is executed and the depth and length of the inclination of the head. Always executed from the waist with the hands by the side, the bow conveys different expressions, such as greeting, apology, gratitude, humility, respect, or remorse. Note that in Asia it is considered impolite to make eye contact while bowing. It might convey distrust. (I do not dare take my eyes off you!) Bowing generally is a body language all by itself in East Asia.

Cheek kissing

Kissing the cheek is a very common form of greeting in Southern Europe and Latin America. Sometimes both cheeks are kissed; sometimes only one cheek is touched lightly by the lips. The kisses are accompanied by a handshake or by putting one's hands on the other person's shoulders. Women often air-kiss to avoid leaving a trace of lipstick on the greeted person's cheek. Although cheek kissing is a sign of affection, it can also be conceived as an invasion of private space and one should therefore be guided by what the other person does. In Southeast Asia and any other country influenced by Muslim or Hindu culture, cheek kissing—especially a woman—is offensive and must be avoided.

Nodding

Another body language signal involving the head is nodding. The head is bobbed vertically once or several times and the gesture generally conveys approval and consent. However, in Bulgaria and Thailand, nodding means the opposite: a very definite "no." Vigorous nodding usually means strong approval, whereas nodding slowly several times can convey, "Maybe, but I'll have to think about it."

ETHICS

So what is ethics? In my simplest definition, it is doing the right thing according to your culture and values. It is making decisions that you believe are right in your world. These are based on your background and how you were raised. It includes your family and your peers. It might include your religion and your culture.

Your background and how you grew up impact your life forever both positively and negatively. If you grew up in a barely subsistence household where food and rent were at a premium, that awareness stays with you for most of your life. If you grew up working in a family setting where work was a pleasant experience, that too stays for life. If you grew up in a multifamily household where elders were honored and respected, that passes on. There's an old folk song that says, "I wanna be like you, Dad." What you were taught matters.

Same goes with peers—who you associate with impacts who you are and who you will become. If all your friends party hardy and think school is lame, guess what? That too is passed on. In order to fit in, you have to be like them.

Culture is also in the mix. A Native American friend of mine told me that it wasn't wrong in his family and tribe to steal from "White People" because they had stolen so much from them, but it was wrong to get caught. True Story.

We all have to make decisions involving our values every day. For example, you order at a fast-food place, and discover as you pull onto the street that you have been given a $10 bill instead of a $1 bill. Do you immediately go back to rectify the mistake, go back the next day, or forget it as it would be inconvenient and the loss is to a large fast-food chain?

Many time ethics does involve money but not always. Some people say that it's easier to make that decision if you have money in your pocket. Maybe, maybe not. There are a lot of examples of street people and the very needy who have turned in both money and valuables to the police. Then what's the link?

In the workplace, it isn't about money most of the time. It's usually about other people's behavior on the job; other people's values that impact your own values. A good example is seeing a friend and colleague put a laptop in his car and then denies any knowledge of ever seeing it. Do you confront him? Tell your supervisor? Forget about it and say that it's none of your business?

Another example is being offered a good paying job with a company that has a reputation for shady dealings. Do you take the job? Do you turn down the job and tell them why? Do you lie and tell them thanks but you've taken another job? What about when your supervisor is behaving in an inappropriate way to a person in an inferior position? Do you call him on it? Talk to him? Protect yourself? What then?

All the above depends on a multitude of factors; they all interplay as to how you value each situation. Remember the second chapter and Maslow's hierarchy of needs? Add your culture and ethnicity, religion, peers and family, and mix in your childhood. Now figure out how each of those has impacted you both positively and negatively. That's how you got the values and ethics you have now. Simple, huh? Yeah, Right!

Age

New research into the medical mysteries of the teenage brain surprised even researchers with their findings. Conventional wisdom has long held that our brains are largely developed by puberty. However, research in the past 10 to 15 years has shown that our brains continue to develop in fundamental ways through the teen years and even into the late 20s and 30s. In fact, Jensen argues in her new book, *The Teenage Brain: A Neuroscientist's Survival Guide to Raising Adolescents and Young Adults*, the teenage years comprise one of the brain's most critical periods for development—likely every bit as crucial as early childhood. "Those seven years in their life is, in a way, as important as their first seven years of life," Jensen says. "It is probably one of the most important seven-year [periods] in their entire life." When I was younger, I thought differently from the way I do today. So, is it any wonder we have different ethics when we're younger? If the brain is not fully developed, it will probably think differently than someone who is older.

Socioeconomic factors

Do socioeconomic factors have anything to do with ethics? For example, if you have a family and your children are starving and you have exhausted all other avenues (work, charity, public works projects), is it a crime to steal food for them? You need to have empathy and put yourself in someone else's shoes. Most people would say it is still stealing. It's hard to judge if you've never been in survival mode. Just ask the 90-year-olds how the Great Depression changed them.

A friend says he listens to the little voice in his head, his conscience. Conscience is a self-perception of right and wrong. If we go back to ethics taught by someone, my conscience is certainly not the same as the mafia mob boss or Mother Teresa's for that matter. Using Maslow's hierarchy of needs, do we have to develop to a certain level of behavior in order to attain a high level of conscience? How about in wars; does the conscience get suppressed or does it cause other longer-term problems for us? Does this experience impact our everyday lives? Follow us to the workplace? Food for thought.

LEADERSHIP

m00osfoto/Shutterstock, Inc.

Ok, this should be our last section, I think, maybe. So what is leadership? According to conventional wisdom, it is the process of leading.

"Control is not leadership; management is not leadership; leadership is leadership. If you seek to lead, invest at least 50% of your time in leading yourself—your own purpose, ethics, principles, motivation, conduct. Invest at least 20% leading those with authority over you and 15% leading your peers." — Dee Hock, Founder and CEO Emeritus, Visa

Think of some of the leaders you have known. Why were they leaders? What was their leadership style? Was their style hard or soft? Let's examine this a little bit. A hard leadership style for me is one who rules on authority. It is their way or the highway. This leadership style is one many people think of as "old school." Indeed, many of the leaders we can think of throughout history have used this leadership style. Did Genghis Khan stop to have a meeting before he sent his warriors into battle? I don't recall seeing that in any of the history books.

This hard leadership style is not all bad. It works well when we have an inexperienced workforce. It also works well when there is an unmotivated group. These groups may need the firm hand of a manager who tells them what to do every second. Another term for this type of manager might be a micromanager. Now, don't get me wrong, when I am at work this style of management drives me crazy. But that is more a reflection of me and my work ethic. I don't feel I need this type of manager in order to get my work done. This type of management style, though, works especially well in situations like the military where top-down leadership is essential for success.

The other type of manager is the soft manager. This manger is more into managing the work flow than the people themselves. The manager treats employees like human beings rather than like interchangeable parts. This manager is concerned with the company's employees and makes sure their physical and emotional needs are met. This manager holds meetings and listens to employees' opinions, even reverting decisions when necessary. Most people would choose this type of manager if asked.

However, all is not perfect in the soft manager's world. This style does not work under many situations. If there is a time-oriented project where stress is rampant, this manager is not an effective leader. In the military where to hesitate may be hazardous, this manager is not effective. If this manager has employees who are self-motivated, then all will probably be fine. However, if the employees are not motivated, then problems with loyalty will likely arise. Workers love this type of manager, but the boss who worries about the bottom line may not.

So, what type of leader should you be? The answer will depend on several factors. Of course, as mentioned before, it will depend on what type of employees you will be leading. A good leader is able to adapt to different circumstances, and tailor their style to that. What is liable to happen is you will have both types, motivated and unmotivated, in your workplace. This means you may have to adjust to each person.

Have you ever been a coach of a sport's team? Sure, as a coach you want to treat everyone the same, but in reality you have to tailor your coaching to each player. Some players will react well to the mean, gruff coach. Think of every movie's image of the gruff but lovable football coach. There will be a point in the movie though, where the coach shows his heart and helps the player who is having problems. This is what happens in reality. Not every person will react well to the hard leadership style. Some will respond better to the soft style.

Another thing that will have an impact on your leadership style is your personality. According to my department chair, we all have the different traits of leadership in us. It is just that we have a natural preference on how you want things to be. So, inside of you is both the hard and soft style. Your natural style will come to the fore when you are placed in a leadership environment. However, you may have to switch styles depending on the people you are leading. For myself, I prefer to use the softer style in most of my classes. However, if the circumstances demand it, I can be the hard leader where I will tell people to sit down and be quiet so other people can learn. I don't particularly like to have to do that, but I can if I need to.

And lastly

I know, I know, I said the last section was the last, so I lied, sue me. A few final thoughts are in order I feel. First off, I hope this book helps you in your search for the perfect job. I wrote it because, #1 the publishers asked me if I would. #2 I had a lot of knowledge I wanted to impart to someone else, and #3 I can get published.

DISCUSSION QUESTIONS

1. Discuss some areas of potential conflicts in communications between different cultures.
2. Name three body language gestures that are interpreted differently in different parts of the world.
3. What are the links between ethics, culture, and economics?
4. What are the pros and cons of each basic leadership style?

TERMS TO REMEMBER

Diversity	Conscience	Multicultural
Ethics	Soft leadership	Hard leadership

THINGS TO REMEMBER

- What's right in your world may not be right in mine.
- Communication is key to understanding.
- You will find your own leadership style.
- You are growing and changing.

REFERENCES

Cheek Kissing Image: Jean Honore Fragonard/Public Domain/commons.wikimedia.org/wiki/File:Jean_Honore_Fragonard_The_Stolen_Kiss.jpg

Bowing Image: Paul Synnott/commons.wikimedia.org/wiki/File:Female_bowing_to_whale.jpg/creativecommons.org/licenses/by/2.0/deed.en

Nod Image: Infrogmation/Public Domain/commons.wikimedia.org/wiki/File:WaitingForYouPost-card1909.JPG

Morris, Desmond. (1994). Bodytalk: The meaning of human gestures.

McNeill, David. (2005). *Gesture and thought.* Chicago: University of Chicago Press.

CPSIA information can be obtained at www.ICGtesting.com
Printed in the USA
LVOW02s0340110615

441966LV00002B/2/P

9 781465 269546